# THE PILGRIM'S PATH

# THE PILGRIM'S PATH

Walking God's Chosen Way for Sanctification and Growth

By Ryan Habbena

Strong Tower Publishing

Bellefonte, PA

www.strongtowerpublishing.com

ISBN 978-0-9822957-3-1

LCCN: 2010938031

# TABLE OF CONTENTS

# INTRODUCTION

Why another book on sanctification? You can walk into any Christian bookstore or seminary library and find sections filled with works on sanctification and spiritual growth. Can anything fresh be written on a subject that has been addressed by thousands of Christian thinkers throughout the centuries?

Many—if not the majority—of these books focus on the *what* of sanctification. There is nothing wrong with such writings, as they serve their intended purpose. We need to know what sanctification looks like and explore its many facets. Indeed, a sizable portion of this work is devoted to this. What I have found lacking, though, is a clear biblical answer to *how* we are called to participate in sanctification. For sure, many establish that we participate, but the concrete, practical *how* is all too frequently missing. Often times, when the how is brought up, it is so far removed from the biblical teachings regarding our participation in the purifying purposes of God that it would have been more beneficial for the reader (and the writer for that matter) that the pen was never picked up at all.

The seeds of this book were sown when I wrote an essay for a scholarship in seminary. The central theme of the paper was "How We Walk by the Spirit." The paper got a strong, positive response from both professors and pastors. This encouraged me to continue to develop the central principles of that paper into this book. The overall focus of the book consists of interacting with foundational texts and, in considering the whole counsel of God, coming to a scriptural worldview regarding the process of sanctification. In light of this, through careful exposition, the goal is to establish several practical conclusions regarding our calling in the quest for conformity to the image of Christ. In essence, the goal is to answer the question, "How do we walk by the Spirit"?

In the church, there has been a morphing emphasis over the last several centuries regarding our relationship to God and our walk with Him. The Reformation brought a renewed vigor for the sovereign grace of God. The Puritans placed an emphasis on our sinfulness and dire need for the grace of God to mortify sin. In the mid-twentieth century, there was a revolution in pursuing the knowledge of God and a subsequent emphasis on the experience of God. It is my conviction that a balanced view is needed that draws upon the rich heritage of solid teaching that has gone before us. However, regarding our beliefs of sanctification and the prescriptions to pursue such, first and foremost, it must be thoroughly scriptural. I pray this work emulates such.

While the central focus of this book is how to walk by the Spirit so that we do not fulfill the desires of the flesh, I believe these pages also provide a much needed reaffirmation of the immediate and critical needs necessary for the corporate church to press on in our calling. Our contemporary Christian climate has too often replaced repentance with relevance, sanctification with life enhancement, and the Scriptures with man-made wisdom. I am convinced that the biblical precepts set forth in this book are the central framework by which we pursue conformity to the image of Christ, both individually and corporately. It is alarming how quickly these foundational truths are being discarded in our contemporary culture.

With this as a primer, let us press forward and explore the gracious yet challenging path God has carved for all His pilgrims.

Beloved, I beg you as sojourners and pilgrims, abstain from fleshly lusts which war against the soul.

1 Peter 2:11 NKJV

# 1

# THE PILGRIM'S PATH

*The Divine Call to Sanctification and Spiritual Growth*

We are pilgrims. We are sojourners caught in an epic conflict. The central front in this ongoing war is our allegiance and obedience to the King of Kings. The inspired pen of the apostle Peter notes our position and proclaims our purpose in this battle:

> Beloved, I beg you as sojourners and pilgrims, abstain from fleshly lusts which war against the soul. (1 Peter 2:11 NKJV)

Those who have walked the "pilgrim's path" for more than a few steps are well acquainted with this raging conflict. To be sure, it is *because* we are pursuing holiness that we are engaged in this intense battle. While we are pressed in on all sides, we have indeed been granted "everything pertaining to life and godliness" (2 Peter 1:3). In light of this comforting yet challenging truth, it is of utmost importance that we understand and avail ourselves of the provisions God has granted His people to walk His divinely decreed way.

11

## PARTAKING IN THE GRAND PILGRIMAGE

When one believes in the person and work of Jesus Christ, he becomes a pilgrim. No longer constituents of "this world," as the author of Hebrews eloquently notes, those who believe have come "to Mount Zion and to the city of the living God, the heavenly Jerusalem, and to myriads of angels, to the general assembly and church of the firstborn who are enrolled in heaven" (Heb. 12:22–23). When we believe, we join the saints of all ages as constituents of Christ's kingdom, forging ahead to our eternal destination. This pilgrimage is grand one, expanding throughout the ages but focused on a singular goal—conformity to the image of Christ.

There is a motif in the pilgrim's journey that runs throughout the Scriptures. Abraham was called out of the idolatrous land of Ur to journey to the Promised Land. The children of Israel were redeemed by the blood of the Lamb and journeyed from Egypt through the wilderness to the threshold of this land. On the grand scale, all those who have been called out of slavery to sin, who are called to flee the worship of vain things, are likewise embarking upon a journey. The journey is from wretchedness to glory. It is us being conformed to the image of Christ and pressing forward to His eternal kingdom. As pilgrims, we join the community of all the ages in fixing our eyes toward journey's end. All believers are partakers.

Again, the author of Hebrews establishes this, noting those who have gone before us:

> All these died in faith, without receiving the
> promises, but having seen them and having

welcomed them from a distance, and having confessed that they were strangers and pilgrims on the earth. For those who say such things make it clear that they are seeking a country of their own . . . And all these, having gained approval through their faith, did not receive what was promised, because God had provided something better for us, so that apart from us they would not be made perfect. (Heb. 11:13–14, 39–40)

When we are placed on the pilgrim's path, we become part of a larger pursuit. We become partakers in a grand marathon that consists of the redeemed of all ages, from the great to the small, striving for conformity to the image of Christ.

## MY BEGINNING

I can vividly recall my initial steps on this path of pilgrims. It was ripened autumn during my first year of college. I had been confronted with gospel, believed in Jesus of Nazareth, and was thirsty for His Word. With so many fresh concepts stirring in my mind, I sought solitude, a place where I could retreat to be alone with Him through prayer and the Word.

Outside of town, there was beautiful haven for those who sought refuge for prayer and reflection. There was a deeply wooded park, which at that time of year was lavished with a glorious spectrum of fall foliage. A winding stone staircase led down to a quiet stream, which had yet another path that weaved its way through a stadium of autumn trees. The end of the path unveiled a towering waterfall that became the centerpiece of the picturesque setting. With the Word clutched by my side, I sat on the shores of the stream, opened my Bible, and began drinking in the goodness of the Word of God.

As I sat there reading the Scriptures, surrounded by the unparalleled artistic power of Lord, I clearly recall not only recognizing with new eyes the outward beauty of creation but inwardly experiencing the initial tastes of the radical, changing power of God's grace. I was taking my first steps on the path to His righteous kingdom. There was a distinct change in my life. There was a stirring in my inner being that had not been roused before. I desired to be conformed to the image of Christ.

Through exploring the Scriptures, I was awakened to the pursuit of holiness. Not only did I read the command to conform to the image of Christ, but this calling was being driven into my heart by the power of the Holy Spirit. I hungered and thirsted for His righteousness.

We all have different stories regarding the origins of our walks in the Lord. While these stories may be different, we all share the same commission powered by a common author. We have been called out of our wretched condition to a glorious transformation. We are a commissioned community, from the saints of old—Noah, Abraham, Isaac, Jacob—to initial stewards of the gospel—Peter, John, James, Paul—to all of those who are walking by His grace today. Spanning the ages and scattered across the globe, we share a common commission of becoming like Him.

## THE STRUGGLE

Although the very beginning of my quest had its
glorious moments, it wasn't always that way. Though
I was awakened to the glories of the Creator and His
Christ, a war was beginning to be waged. The
command to conform was given, the commission
received, and the desire to fulfill was evident. Yet there
was a conflict arising in my life. While my inner man
authentically desired to be conformed to the image of
Christ, I found myself perpetually failing. The conflict
Paul describes in Romans 7 read like my
autobiography:

> For I joyfully concur with the law of God in the
> inner man, but I see a different law in the
> members of my body, waging war against the
> law of my mind and making me a prisoner of the
> law of sin which is in my members. Wretched
> man that I am! Who will set me free from the
> body of this death? (Rom. 7:22–24)

Although I had received the command to conform to
the image of the Christ, the how was unclear to me.
Sanctification was my goal, but sin kept arising—kept
entangling—and frustration set in. As my worldview
became clarified, I came to realize this struggle defines
the quest. The Puritan John Owen wrote extensively
on the struggle against sin, and rightly assesses:

> Every single day the believer finds a conflict
> with sin. Sin is always active, always planning,
> always enticing and tempting. Either sin is
> defeating us or we are defeating it. It will be like
> this until the day we die. There is no safety
> against sin except in constant warfare against it.[1]

15

Although peace with God is accomplished, conflict with evil is created. "I find then the principle that evil is present in me, the one who wants to do good" (Rom. 7:21). The eighteenth century theologian Jonathan Edwards, in preaching a sermon entitled "The Christian Pilgrim," encourages us in the midst of this conflict:

> Though the road be difficult and toilsome, we must hold out with patience, and be content to endure hardships. Though the journey be long, yet we must not stop short; but hold on till we arrive at the place we seek. Nor should we be discouraged with the length and difficulty of the way, as the children of Israel were, and be for turning back again. All our thought and design should be to press forward until we arrive.[2]

As members of the grand community pressing forward on the road of being conformed to the image of Christ, we do well to heed such exhortation. One glorious day, we will cross the finish line and God's ultimate purpose in us will be realized. Until then, we are called to run the race before us.

## THE PILGRIM'S PURSUIT OF HOLINESS

The author of Hebrews further fortifies this call to holiness. In doing so, he establishes the need for all those engaged to run the race. He also clearly defines who will bring this quest to completion.

> Therefore, since we have so great a cloud of witnesses surrounding us, let us also lay aside every encumbrance and the sin which so easily entangles us, and let us run with endurance the

16

race that is set before us, fixing our eyes on
Jesus, the author and finisher of faith. (Heb.
12:1–2)

The call is clear. Any "encumbrance" hindering us
from pursuing our purification must be shaken off.
"The sin which so easily entangles" must be shed.
Fixing our eyes on the Son of God, who is our Chief
Shepherd guiding us to glory, is the way to proceed.
As we run this race, we are surrounded by a "cloud of
witnesses." The author of Hebrews has just described
these fellow pilgrims in chapter eleven. They are those
who have run the race before us. They are the
sojourners who by the power of God have conquered
kingdoms, suffered for the King, and kept the faith.
They are our common partners in seeking the
kingdom. Their lives are witnesses of God's power in
the lives of His pilgrim people. We share a common
road, with a common goal and a collective faith in the
King. At the apex is Jesus, the "author and finisher."
He has provided everything we need. He is the one
who places us on the starting line, who is with us for
every strained and difficult step, and who carries us
across the finish line.

This is not a quiet, isolated call. The call to
sanctification and spiritual growth is a resounding one
that echoes throughout the pages of Scripture. This is
the very reason we are called pilgrims. We are
pursuing a prize, a place, and a Person that are not of
this world. The following trilogy of verses further
stress this high calling.

In writing the Thessalonian church, Paul
proclaims the will of God for them:

> . . . that each of you know how to possess his
> own vessel in sanctification and honor (1 Thess.
> 4:4)

The writer of Hebrews again exhorts the constituents of the kingdom of Christ:

> Pursue peace with all men, and the
> sanctification without which no one will see
> the Lord. (Heb. 12:14)

In the midst of Paul's explanation for the need for the people of God to purge themselves of dishonorable works, he teaches Timothy:

> If anyone cleanses himself from these things, he
> will be a vessel for honor, sanctified, useful to
> the Master, prepared for every good work.
> Now flee from youthful lusts and pursue
> righteousness, faith, love and peace, with those
> who call on the Lord from a pure heart. (2 Tim.
> 2:21–22)

All of these exhortations (seek sanctification, pursue righteousness, strive for holiness) are various ways of expressing our overarching goal: conformity to the image of Christ. Jesus Himself gave us this as a primary pursuit: "Seek first the kingdom of God and His righteousness" (Matt. 6:33).

Since this is what our Lord has commanded and is of the first order, we do well to ask: "What is the kingdom of God?"

## SEEKING THE KINGDOM OF GOD

The kingdom of God speaks of His reign. In the Scriptures, we are taught that when Christ came and accomplished His redemptive work, the kingdom arrived. It is spoken of as a present reality (e.g. Col. 1:13, Rev. 1:6). Yet in other portions of God Word, it is presented as a promised future reality (e.g. 2 Peter 1:11, Gal. 5:21). How do we make sense of this?

With the coming of Christ, the King arrived. If the King had not invaded this world to go to the cross, the kingdom would have been without a constituency. Jesus purchased His kingdom with His passion on the cross, was raised, and is now reigning at the right hand of the Father. His rule is real. His kingdom is an actuality. The kingdom consists of an ascended King and a pilgrim people who believe in His name—now. The Psalms speak of this era of the Messiah's reign: "The Lord will stretch forth Your strong scepter from Zion, saying, 'Rule in the midst of Your enemies'" (Psalm 110:2). Even while we are in the "midst of His enemies," our King is still ruling and all His people are journeying toward the ultimate goal of entering the fullness of His kingdom when He returns.

As pilgrims in this world, we seek the kingdom already by reflecting His righteousness and striving for the characteristics that mark the kingdom of God. But we keep our eyes on the blessed day we enter the fullness of His glory—when He returns—which has not yet transpired. We are progressing in His righteousness and moving ever closer to the time when the kingdom of this world becomes the kingdom of our God and His Christ (Rev. 11:15). As the Scriptures testify, "Salvation is closer now than when we first believed" (Rom. 13:11). We seek the kingdom now by seeking the righteousness of the King.

## THE PILGRIM'S POWER

While we walk this difficult yet blessed path, it is imperative to recognize the source of our progress. In the book of Titus, immediately after calling us to "seek His righteousness," Paul ensures we understand where the power of our purification comes from: "Christ Jesus; who gave Himself for us, that He might redeem us from every lawless deed and purify for Himself a people for His own possession, zealous for good deeds" (Titus 2:14). Charles Spurgeon eloquently exhorts:

> Though you have struggled in vain against your evil habits, though you have wrestled with them sternly, and resolved, and re-resolved, only to be defeated by your giant sins and your terrible passions, there is One who can conquer all your sins for you. There is One who is stronger than Hercules, who can strangle the hydra of your lust, kill the lion of your passions, and cleanse the Augean stable of your evil nature by turning the great rivers of blood and water of his atoning sacrifice right through your soul. He can make and keep you pure within. Oh, look to him![3]

Jesus is the source of purification. Jesus is the warrior who slays sin. Jesus is the Savior who sanctifies our souls. We are to realize, though He has accomplished this task, there is still a path of progress that leads to the consummation of our sanctification. Though our King has authored and finished the work of salvation, He has laid before us a quest.

## THE CALL TO THE QUEST

Throughout the tumultuous times that accompanied my initial steps, I sought to find proper footing. As I continued to explore what the Scriptures proclaimed regarding the pursuit of sanctification, my worldview became more clarified. This life is a struggle as we make our way to the kingdom. Sin is an ever-present foe seeking us ruin. Yet there is indeed victory, peace, contentment, and the truth that we have been granted "everything pertaining to life and godliness through Him who loved us" (2 Peter 1:3). Just as Paul noted our struggle in Romans 7, he bridges this conflict to our victory.

> Thanks be to God through Jesus Christ our Lord! So then, on the one hand I myself with my mind am serving the law of God, but on the other, with my flesh the law of sin. Therefore there is now no condemnation for those who are in Christ Jesus. For the law of the Spirit of life in Christ Jesus has set you free from the law of sin and of death. (Rom. 7:25–8:2)

In my own pilgrimage, while these dynamics became clear, there were still aspects left unanswered. Specifically, I strived for an answer to this central question: *What are we specifically called to practice in order to advance in our quest for sanctification?*

Every pilgrim needs the answer to this question. This book seeks to clarify this important issue through careful consideration of the provision God Himself has proclaimed He has provided for us in this unparalleled pursuit. If we know what He has provided, we can know what He wants us to do and put it into practice.

If you are a believer in Jesus of Nazareth, you have been called to conformity to the image of Christ. This is the inception of a journey. This is a race, a quest. It has its origins before the foundation of the world. It has been extended to us in this life and finds fulfillment in the life to come. We *will* be conformed to the image of Christ. We *will* enter into His eternal kingdom. While there will come a time when we cease to be pilgrims, our endeavors into the depths and riches of our majestic God are eternal.

With these promises in mind, let us proceed to explore the provisions He has granted and be divinely equipped to walk this pilgrim's path.

---

[1] John Owen, *What Every Christian Needs to Know* (London: Grace Publications, 1998), 78–79.

[2] Jonathan Edwards, *Growing in God's Spirit* (Phillipsburg: P&R, 2003), 117.

[3] C. H. Spurgeon, "The Sixth Beatitude," sermon delivered April 27, 1873.

# THE PILGRIM'S PATH

&#x269A;&#x269A;

"Enter through the narrow gate; for the gate is wide and the way is broad that leads to destruction, and there are many who enter through it. For the gate is small and the way is narrow that leads to life, and there are few who find it."

Matthew 7:13–14

# 2

# The Two Gates

*Ensuring We Have Entered the Way of Eternal Life*

There are two gates placed before every human being who walks this earth. Both are entrances to the paths of destiny. While each leads to eternity, the outcomes couldn't be more opposed. One path is broad, the other narrow. One is easy, the other difficult. One is beautiful in the eyes of men, the other offensive. One leads to destruction, the other to life. The archway to the entrance that leads to eternal life reads, "This is the King of the Jews."

The cross of Jesus Christ is the entrance to eternal life. All other ways, no matter how attractive to our eyes, are paths to eternal destruction.

## TO THE CALLED – THE POWER OF GOD

Evidence for the authenticity of the one true gospel is overwhelming when we examine the cross. We read Paul's explanation of the cross and its implications in 1 Corinthians:

> For the word of the cross is to those who are perishing foolishness, but to us who are being

25

saved it is the power of God. For it is written, "I will destroy the wisdom of the wise, and the cleverness of the clever I will set aside." Where is the wise man? Where is the scribe? Where is the debater of this age? Has not God made foolish the wisdom of the world? For since in the wisdom of God the world through its wisdom did not come to know God, God was well-pleased through the foolishness of the message preached to save those who believe. For indeed Jews ask for signs, and Greeks search for wisdom; but we preach Christ crucified, to Jews a stumbling block, and to Gentiles foolishness, but to those who are the called, both Jews and Greeks, Christ the power of God and the wisdom of God. (1 Cor. 1:18–24)

The message of the cross, shorthand for the death and resurrection of Christ and their monumental significance, is by its very nature offensive and foolish to fallen minds. This message proclaims that the violent, shameful death of a man outside the city of Jerusalem is the solution to our ultimate problem. This message proclaims this man was and is the God of creation, the God of Abraham, Isaac, and Jacob. This message takes this bloody, torturous execution and announces it continually to the world. Yet, throughout the ages, the Holy Spirit has freed human hearts to believe this message and draw people to citizenship in the kingdom of Christ.

In light of the inherent foolishness and offense of the cross, and in light of continued expansion of Christ's kingdom through conversions, such truths illuminate the evidence that only God could accomplish such a task.

The message of the cross is offensive and crude. Yet to the called, it is the power of God and the only pathway to the kingdom. This enduring message is the source and continuing central truth in our quest for conformity to the image of Christ.

## OUR ULTIMATE PROBLEM

If we are to engage in any meaningful discussion of salvation, we must first identify what we are being saved from. The ultimate problem of every fallen individual is sin. Sin is both the state and activity of separation from God and His righteous precepts. Through the fall of our first parents and our carrying out of the family tradition of sin, every one of us has violated the law of God and are by nature considered His enemies. Without the intervention of grace, we are destined for wrath.

Paul established these truths in his epistle to the Ephesians.

> You were dead in your trespasses and sins, in which you formerly walked according to the course of this world, according to the prince of the power of the air, of the spirit that is now working in the sons of disobedience. Among them we too all formerly lived in the lusts of our flesh, indulging the desires of the flesh and of the mind, and were by nature children of wrath, even as the rest. (Eph. 2:1–3)

Sin is our greatest problem. Why? Because it has divided us from the God of creation and produced both spiritual and physical death in all of Adam's offspring. Yet the grace of the Lord has intervened.

As Paul continues, "But God, being rich in mercy, because of His great love with which He loved us, even when we were dead in our transgressions, made us alive together with Christ (by grace you have been saved), and raised us up with Him, and seated us with Him in the heavenly places in Christ Jesus" (Eph. 2:4–6). The solution to the problem of sin is the grace of God in Jesus of Nazareth.

## A NECESSARY STARTING POINT

Before any consideration is to be made regarding the means of attaining practical purification, prior to asking questions regarding what we are to do in our quest, and prior to engaging in any exploration into how we are to called to participate in conformity to the image of Christ, we must be sure we have actually entered the one path that produces genuine purification and leads to the everlasting kingdom of Christ. We must be sure we have entered through the narrow gate.

In his classic work on the quest to kill sin, *The Mortification of Sin*, John Owen acknowledges what must be our primary priority:

> What hath been spoken, I suppose is sufficient to make good my first general rule, Be sure to get an interest in Christ, if you intend to mortify any sin; without it, it will never be done.[1]

In order to pursue the ongoing process of sanctification, it is of first order to be sure that the issues of sin, wrath, and judgment have been resolved. While certainly fearful initially (and rightfully so), we must address our standing before the Holy Creator of all. No pursuit of purification will amount to anything if we have not truly entered the path that has been paved by the blood of our Savior. No quest for conformity to the image of Christ will advance if we have not followed the King's central command: *Enter through the narrow gate.*

## The King's Command

In Matthew's account of the life and teachings of Jesus, the apostle records Jesus' instructions in what is known as the Sermon on the Mount. This powerful discourse is the spiritual antidote for pride. The disciples had gathered around Jesus, and He "opened His mouth and began to teach to them" (Matt. 5:2).

In beginning His discourse, Jesus announces His purpose for His earthly ministry: "Do not think that I came to abolish the Law or the Prophets; I did not come to abolish, but to fulfill. For truly I say to you, until heaven and earth pass away, not the smallest letter or stroke shall pass away from the Law, until all is accomplished" (Matt. 5:17–18). The Prophet, the one greater than Moses whom the Lord promised would come and guide His people into His perfect principles (Deut. 18:15), then proceeded to teach the righteous commandments of God.

If this account is carefully read and one's life is assessed in light of it, the King's words convict. Throughout the sermon, Jesus not only affirms the Law but also reveals the intensity of its requirements. In order to fulfill the command to not murder, we must never be angry without proper cause (Matt.

29

5:21–22). In order to fulfill the command to not commit adultery, we must not even look with lustful intentions (Matt. 5:27–28).

Throughout the account, our King continues to establish the radical requirements of our righteous God. He concludes with this command:

> "Enter through the narrow gate; for the gate is wide and the way is broad that leads to destruction, and there are many who enter through it. For the gate is small and the way is narrow that leads to life, and there are few who find it." (Matt. 7:13)

Since these are the authoritative words of the Son of God, let us discern whether or not we have truly entered through the one gate that leads to life.

## THE WIDE AND NARROW GATES

Jesus paints a clear contrast. Enter through the narrow gate or walk the broad path that leads to destruction. We have examined the narrow gate, but what is the broad path? As we examine the context and intent of Matthew's account, it becomes apparent that Jesus is drawing the proverbial line that divides all of humanity. If one does not gather under His kingship and His alone, he is proceeding on the path of destruction. Just what does walking this way entail?

In describing the wide gate and broad path, Jesus is using powerful imagery that conveys that if one does not trust Him and His Word, they are *by default* on the path to destruction. For "he who does not believe has been judged already, because he has not believed in the name of the only begotten Son of God" (John 3:18). If one's heart and mind are not fixed on the true and living Christ, that person is not trusting God's one and only provision for salvation. This is as true for us as it was for the initial hearers who sat at Jesus' feet.

Recall the context of the command to enter the narrow gate. It follows the intense requirements of the Law. If one is to be saved, these requirements must be met. We may conduct a search into the thousands of religious rites that exist in this world. We may delve into the millions of teachings that have been set forth promising eternal life and freedom for this cursed existence. We may explore all of human history intensely, scanning the billions who have walked this earth. Only one has the solution. Only one has fulfilled the Law entirely. Only one has proven Himself the true Messiah of God. Only one has sacrificed Himself to save the world. Only one has been raised, authenticating all His claims. *He* is the narrow gate.

Many have attempted to lessen the impact of Jesus' teachings and the essential need for every human to have the Law fulfilled on their behalf. However, not only does Jesus affirm this truth through His teachings, but the Holy Spirit testifies to such through Paul in his exhortation in Romans.

> For what the Law could not do, weak as it was through the flesh, God did: sending His own Son in the likeness of sinful flesh and as an offering for sin, He condemned sin in the flesh, in order that the requirement of the Law might be fulfilled in us, who do not walk according to the flesh, but according to the Spirit. (Rom. 8:3–4)

31

So the *what* of what we are called to do is established. We must enter through the gate that Jesus has established. No matter how appealing to the senses or how compelling an alternative may seem, any path other than His path is the way of destruction.

The English expositor Martin Lloyd Jones further comments on this passage, noting:

> He has not merely come to save us from punishment and from hell; He has come to make us holy, and "purify unto himself a peculiar people, zealous of good works." He came into this world to prepare the way of holiness, and His ambition and His purpose for us is that we shall walk in the way in His steps, in this high calling, in this glorious life, that we should even as He Himself lived it, resisting even to blood if necessary. That was His life, a straight and thorny road, but He trod it. And your privilege and mine is the privilege of coming out of the world and entering into this life, following Him all the way.[2]

So how do we enter through this narrow gate and walk this narrow path that leads to life? The answer for all is the same: through faith.

## BECOMING A CHILD OF ABRAHAM

Four thousand years ago, in a world ripe with paganism, God singled out one man, Abraham. God's sovereign choice was made to continue the promise of redemption and demonstrate how He saves. Abraham has rightly been called "the father of the faithful." In the person of Abraham, we behold a portrait of how salvation is achieved: by trusting God and His provision. All who, like Abraham, place their trust in God and His provision are considered His children. In the book of Galatians, we read:

> Abraham believed God, and it was reckoned to him as righteousness. Therefore, be sure that it is those who are of faith who are sons of Abraham. The Scripture, foreseeing that God would justify the Gentiles by faith, preached the gospel beforehand to Abraham, saying, "All the nations will be blessed in you." So then those who are of faith are blessed with Abraham, the believer. (Gal. 3:6–9)

Abraham believed the provision and promise of God and walked according to His commands. We now have the gospel announced to us. The promise has been fulfilled and the one message by which humans are saved from sin has been delivered once for all. The person and work of Jesus Christ is the only provision that leads to life. Faith in Him and His finished work is the means of being justified before the heavenly courts. Rather than being legal fiction, this is historic reality. Trusting Jesus and following His Word is entering through the narrow gate. Jesus challenged His contemporaries with this one indisputable declaration that divides all of humanity: "If you were Abraham's children do the deeds of Abraham" (John 8:39). All who, like Abraham, refuse to bow to the surrounding religions of man and instead submit to the one true God and His provision for salvation are His children and will inherit the eternal blessing.

The narrow and wide gates are decisively encapsulated in the following wisdom found in book Jeremiah:

> Thus says the Lord, "Cursed is the man who
> trusts in mankind and makes flesh his strength,
> and whose heart turns away from the Lord. . . .
> Blessed is the man who trusts in the Lord and
> whose trust is the Lord." (Jer. 17:5, 7)

The wide gate of "trusting man" is our default position. It is how we are born. We are born in sin and under the Law. Therefore, we are cursed. We are born bent towards trusting our own abilities and nature. There are millions of different precepts to which one may adhere regarding God, eternity, and the afterlife. If one hears the message of the gospel and refuses, that person is trusting that the gospel is not true. Consequently, whatever this person does trust is irrelevant. If one's trust is not centered on the person and work of Jesus Christ, he finds himself on the broad and easy path that leads to destruction.

In summarizing the essence of the broad and narrow gates, John MacArthur states:

> There may be a thousand different religions in names and terms, but only two religions really exist. There is the truth of divine accomplishment, which says God has done it all in Christ, and there is the lie of human achievement, which says we have some sort of hand in saving ourselves. One is the religion of grace, the other is the religion of works. One offers salvation by faith alone; the other offers salvation by the flesh.[3]

When confronted with the gospel, we are presented with the narrow gate of trusting the provision of the Lord. We are presented with the extremely narrow proclamation that one man with one message holds

34

the solution to the ultimate problem of the desolate race of humanity.

## THE SAVIOR'S SOLUTION

From the inception of sin in the Garden of Eden, God has announced His solution. The Serpent tempted, humanity caved, and sin and death reigned down upon the earth. Through the bleak and dark cloud, the promise of the Lord pierced: "The Lord God said to the serpent, 'Because you have done this, cursed are you more than all cattle, and more than every beast of the field; on your belly you will go, and dust you will eat all the days of your life; and I will put enmity between you and the woman, and between your seed and her seed; He shall bruise you on the head, and you shall bruise him on the heel" (Gen. 3:14–15).

In essence, the solution to the problem that began in the Garden, incited by the Serpent, would find its solution in the Seed of the woman. In His sovereign wisdom, the Lord set in motion the promise that would weave its way through human history until a young Jewish virgin was found to be with Child. "When the fullness of the time came, God sent forth His Son, born of a woman" (Gal. 4:16).

In order to fulfill the requirements of the Law, Jesus walked in the "likeness of sinful flesh" (Rom. 8:3). He was, and is, true God and true man. Yet He shouldered the burden of mortal existence to become the perfect sacrifice: to trade His righteous, pure life for our wretched, perverse one. The transaction took place on a tree. He took our punishment and gave us His grace. As the sovereign Lord of creation, the

35

eternal King of the house of David hung bleeding on the cross of Calvary and secured the power to forever purge sin and its dastardly consequences. He announced His triumph: "It is finished," breathed His last breaths in His unglorified body, and died. Three days later, He pierced the darkness of death by becoming the first of a multitude from every tribe, nation, and tongue to experience the resurrection of the dead. It was impossible for death to hold Him.

Today is the day of salvation. In Christ, we have seen the Conqueror of sin and beheld the promise of what all who believe in Him will become. His message soars to ends of the earth calling out to all: "Repent and believe the good news!"

Jesus is the solution to sin. He holds the purifying potency to conquer the penalty, power, and presence of sin. We must listen. We must heed how the King of Kings requires us to respond to His redemptive calling. We must repent of our sins, turning from sin, self, and Satan. We must trust the person and work of Jesus Christ. Then and only then may we proceed with the commissioned task of entering the path that leads to the life and allowing ourselves to be conformed to His image.

## GOSPEL-DRIVEN SANCTIFICATION

We must be careful not to view the task of conforming to the image of Christ as something we must do to earn or remain in God's favor. This thought may be subtle in the believer's mind, and it is easy to fall into this erroneous way of thinking. Jerry

Bridges exhorts us to pursue sanctification, being established by the grace of the gospel:

> Perhaps no one apart from Jesus himself has ever been as committed a disciple in both life and ministry as the Apostle Paul. Yet he did not look to his own performance but to Christ's performance as the sole basis of his acceptance with God. So I learned that Christians need to hear the gospel all of their lives because it is the gospel that continues to remind us that our day-to-day acceptance with the Father is not based on what we do for God but upon what Christ did for us in his sinless life and sin-bearing death. I began to see that we stand before God today as righteous as we will ever be, even in heaven, because he has clothed us with the righteousness of his Son.[4]

Being girded with gratitude for the grace that has been given to us, we can forge ahead on the pilgrim's path.

Once we can respond affirmatively to question, "Have you entered through the narrow gate?" and know we have been gifted with the Shepherd of our souls who walks with us every step of the path, our next task is to map the quest that has been laid before us.

---

[1] John Owen, *The Mortification of Sin* (Ross-Shire: Christian Focus Publications, 2002), 84.

[2] Martyn Lloyd-Jones, *Studies in the Sermon on the Mount* (Grand Rapids: Eerdmans, 1960), 485.

[3] John MacArthur, *Hard to Believe* (Nashville: Thomas Nelson, 2003), 78-79

---

[4] Jerry Bridges, "Gospel-Driven Sanctification" *Modern Reformation* (May / June Issue, Vol. 12.3), p. 14.

# THE TWO GATES

❧❧

Not that I have already obtained it or have already become perfect, but I press on so that I may lay hold of that for which also I was laid hold of by Christ Jesus.

Philippians 3:12

3

# Mapping the Quest

*Charting the Course of Conformity to the Image of Christ*

I'm sure you have heard of the exploits of the infamous explorer Ponce De Leon. De Leon was commissioned by his home country of Spain to obtain a rather elusive prize. There was a legend, most probably overheard from the natives, of an island called Bemini. This island was said to be a lush garden holding vast riches and a fountain flowing with the power to provide perpetual youth and health. De Leon carefully considered the course, planned accordingly, and launched his quest. He endured severe weather, hostile forces, and other hindrances to in the pursuit of his goal. As you may be aware, De Leon's quest ended in failure. Not only did he fail to find unending youth and riches, but he died by the arrows of fighting natives. Although he meticulously mapped his course and braved the stormy seas, his journey consummated in a tidal wave of failure.

In contrast, for those who have entered through the narrow gate will be met with victory. The certain treasure that awaits the end of our quest is an authentic, unending fountain of eternal life.

Like the seasoned adventurers of yesteryear, we also must map our quest to the kingdom. Our worldview must be established. We must know what to expect. We must know who and what may oppose us. We must ascertain when and where our quest will find its consummation.

So let us unroll the map, found in the guiding Word of God, which has been the compass for the commissioned community throughout the ages.

## KNOW THY ENEMY

As we look to chart the course of conformity to the image of Christ, we find this path to be surrounded by enemies. First among them are Satan and his hordes.

When we believe in Christ, this spiritual host become our sworn enemy. Its goal is to prevent us from progressing. While much of the angelic and spiritual realm remains a mystery, we are informed that Satan and his minions seek to corrupt and destroy the commissioned children of God. The apostle Peter plainly apprises us of this reality:

> Be of sober spirit, be on the alert. Your adversary, the devil, prowls around like a roaring lion, seeking someone to devour. But resist him, firm in your faith, knowing that the same experiences of suffering are being accomplished by your brethren who are in the world. (1 Peter 5:8–9)

The enemy is on the prowl and seeking to devour. We are to be alert and resist him, being firmly planted in what Christ, our Warrior, has accomplished. We must recognize this reality but also be careful not to place our focus on the angelic realm. Christ has conquered the principalities and powers for us, so we need not fear nor focus on them.

C. S. Lewis has granted a nugget of wisdom regarding our outlook on the spiritual powers that oppose our progression. In the preface to his fiction work *The Screwtape Letters*, he well notes: "There are two equal and opposite errors into which our race can fall about the devils. One is to disbelieve their existence. The other is to believe, and to feel an excessive and unhealthy interest in them. They themselves are equally pleased by both errors."[1] We are to recognize, resist, and keep running the race, fixing our eyes not on those who wish to thwart us but on our Redeemer, who has gone before us and secured our salvation.

Another force that seeks to hinder our progress is the world. We are surrounded by a climate of corruption that will continually seek to pull Christ's pilgrims into its seductive grasp. In describing our fallen surroundings, the apostle John notes:

> For all that is in the world, the lust of the flesh and the lust of the eyes and the boastful pride of life, is not from the Father, but is from the world. The world is passing away, and also its lusts; but the one who does the will of God lives forever. (1 John 2:16–17)

John goes on to describe those who are victorious:

> For whatever is born of God overcomes the world; and this is the victory that has overcome the world—our faith . . . We know that we are of God, and that the whole world lies in the power of the evil one. (1 John 5:4, 19)

We are walking toward a world that will be renewed, and the cursed, corrupting influences that surround us will be forever removed. But in order to progress, we must recognize and resist the fallen, corrupt climate that seeks to entangle us.

With these being noted, we are now forced to look at our most dangerous foe. This foe is deceptive, treacherous, and constantly seeking ruin. He presses in on all sides. Surprisingly, this dangerous enemy is not Satan but another corrupt character who is always near—the old self.

When the Holy Spirit floods the believer's being with new life through faith, he becomes a new creation. A new person is "birthed" who thirsts for righteousness, truth, and purity. Along with this, a conflict is created. An old enemy remains whose desires are in conflict with this new creation. When the first buds of regeneration sprout, a battle for our hearts and minds begins. This enemy—the old self—lurks within us, always present, and seeks to slow the progress of sanctification.

The inspired Word of God sketches this conflict using the imagery of two separate natures now residing in the same body. In Colossians 3, Paul exhorts those chosen by God to proceed in shedding the old and putting on the new:

> Do not lie to one another, since you laid aside the old self with its evil practices, and have put on the new self who is being renewed to a true knowledge according to the image of the One who created him. (Col. 3:9–10)

Through belief in Christ, we have "laid aside" the old self, our unredeemed nature and all its destructive practices. We have put on the "new self," which is being renewed according to the image of Christ.[2] The old self was destroyed at the cross. In Romans, we are taught, in light of the redemptive work of Christ, as follows: "[K]nowing this, that our old self was crucified with Him, in order that our body of sin might be done away with, so that we would no longer be slaves to sin" (Rom. 6:6).

Though this occurred once for all through the redemptive work of Christ (and our reception of His power through faith), this conflict is continuing as we progress in our sanctification. Paul utilizes this same imagery in Ephesians.

> But you did not learn Christ in this way, if indeed you have heard Him and have been taught in Him, just as truth is in Jesus, that, in reference to your former manner of life, you lay aside the old self, which is being corrupted in accordance with the lusts of deceit, and that you be renewed in the spirit of your mind, and put on the new self, which in the likeness of God has been created in righteousness and holiness of the truth. (Eph. 4:20–24)

So we are called to continually lay aside our old self and put on the new self. The old self is entirely opposed to God and His purposes. It cannot be reasoned with, it cannot be reformed, it cannot be redeemed. It can only be put to death. As it is put to death, a new person is being unveiled, one who is united with the eternal righteousness of Jesus Christ. This is the foundational conflict that defines the course.

## TWO PRECEPTS OF PURIFICATION

As we progress from the narrow gate to the consummation of our redemption, we are undergoing a divinely initiated purification. This purification has two integrated yet distinct precepts: *mortification* and *vivification*.

Paul often utilizes the word "flesh" (Gr. *sarx*) to describe our fallen, sinful nature. All those who are reborn are continually, by the sovereign power of God, putting to death this inner foe. The term for this is *mortification*, meaning "to execute, to put to death, to destroy." We are informed:

> So then, brethren, we are under obligation, not to the flesh, to live according to the flesh—for if you are living according to the flesh, you must die; but if by the Spirit *you are putting to death the deeds of the body*, you will live. (Rom. 8:12–13, emphasis mine)

We are further exhorted:

> *Put to death* therefore what is earthly in you: sexual immorality, impurity, passion, evil desire, and covetousness, which is idolatry. On account of these the wrath of God is coming. (Col. 3:5–6, emphasis mine)

We are divinely commanded to execute, through the grace that is given us, the desires of the old self. We are called to plunge our divinely bestowed weapons into our corrupt nature and continually put to death the rebellious child of Adam residing in all of us. John Owen coined a phrase that expresses the necessity of this execution: "Be killing sin or sin will be killing you."[3]

As we progress on this path, we can look back and see the shedding of this foe through mortification, but we also forge forward in newness of life, marching forth through *vivification*.

Jerry Bridges well explains these complimentary truths:

> Just as it is "by the Spirit" that we put to death the misdeeds of the body so it is by the Spirit that we put on the virtues of Christlike character. That is why Paul could say in Colossians 3:12–14 that we are to clothe ourselves with these qualities (emphasizing our responsibility), while Galatians 5:22–23 he refers to Christian character traits as the "fruit of the Spirit" (emphasizing our dependence on the Spirit). The same Spirit who enables us to mortify sin also enables us to put on godly character.[4]

While mortification describes what we are destroying, vivification describes what we are becoming. They are the two sides of the same coin of purification.

## PARADOXES OF PURIFICATION

The term *sanctification*, as found in the Scriptures, is foundationally defined as being "set apart." It is intimately tied to the truth of being selected for service and obedience unto God. As we explore the biblical concept of sanctification, we discover a proclamation of the sure nature of our quest, but also an implicit call to participate in its glorious unfolding.

When teaching us the reality of sanctification, the picture painted by the Scriptures is one of paradox.

Throughout the whole counsel of God, there is vast teaching proclaiming the finished reality of sanctification. This truth is tied to the sacrifice of the great High Priest, Jesus. Through His once-for-all propitiation, He purified us, therefore sanctifying us. This radical redemption is clearly taught in Hebrews:

> By this will we have been sanctified through the offering of the body of Jesus Christ once for all . . . For by one offering He has perfected for all time those who are sanctified. (Heb. 10:10,14)

Yet there is also a stream of inspired teaching that proclaims that sanctification, being set apart from self and sin to serve the living God, is an ongoing process. Note Paul's concluding prayer in 1 Thessalonians:

> Now may the God of peace Himself sanctify you entirely; and may your spirit and soul and body be preserved complete, without blame at the coming of our Lord Jesus Christ. Faithful is He who calls you, and He also will bring it to pass. (1 Thess. 5:17–18)

So our sanctification is both a completed task and an ongoing process. It has been completed and is being accomplished. How do we make sense of these seemingly conflicting principles?

The cross of Christ has sanctified us "once for all" and "perfected us for all time." Yet the Lord in His sovereign wisdom is applying this sanctification to us through a process. These two streams of scriptural teaching are not establishing opposing aspects of purification. Rather they are establishing intimate— indeed, inseparable—precepts. J. C. Ryle provides a suitable definition that includes both:

> Sanctification is that inward spiritual work
> which the Lord Jesus Christ works in a man by
> the Holy Spirit, when He calls him to be a true
> believer. He not only washes him from his sins
> in His own blood, but He also separates him
> from his natural love of sin and the world, puts
> a new principle in his heart and makes him
> practically godly in life.[5]

Our sanctification was secured once for all on the cross. It *was accomplished*. Through the renewing power of the Holy Spirit, this sanctification *is being applied* to our lives. Since our Savior has already secured our sanctification, through faith we have begun the race and are journeying from wretchedness to glory. As noted previously, we are called to engage in this process.

## PERFECTION: WHEN?

A question regarding sanctification that is often asked is this: "Are we able to achieve a state of perfection before we enter glory?" While some have answered this question in the affirmative, both the Scriptures and history speak against such. While there are those who have taught this precept, and even those who audaciously claimed to have achieved this state, a couple of basic observations nullify this possibility.

While we are to press on towards this goal, our fallen flesh remains a reality. This will be a continual conflict until we shed this mortal body and put on immortality. In fact, John notes that the thinking of our sinlessness before the appointed time is a product of self-deception. "If we say that we have no sin, we are deceiving ourselves, and the truth is not in us" (1

John 1:8). Paul exemplified the attitude of looking towards the promise of complete sanctification but regarding oneself with a truthful assessment:

> *Not that I have already obtained it, or have already become perfect,* but I press on in order that I may lay hold of that for which also I was laid hold of by Christ Jesus. Brethren, I do not regard myself as having laid hold of it yet; but one thing I do: forgetting what lies behind and reaching forward to what lies ahead, I press on toward the goal for the prize of the upward call of God in Christ Jesus. (Phil. 3:12–14, emphasis mine)

Beyond this, there is another paradox at work on the path of purity. We may often think that the more we advance, the more righteous we will feel. In fact, the inverse is true. The closer we come to the Light of the Lord, the more we become aware of the stains of our sin. When we read the accounts of those who were closely confronted with the Holy One, they were highly conscious of their own wretchedness.

When the prophet Isaiah approached the throne of God, his contrite response to the divine presence was: "Woe is me, for I am ruined! Because I am a man of unclean lips, and I live among a people of unclean lips; for my eyes have seen the King, the Lord of hosts" (Isa. 6:5). Likewise Job, the one whom the Lord declared had no equal on the earth, responded when encountering the holy Lord of all: "I have heard of You by the hearing of the ear; but now my eye sees You; therefore I retract, and I repent in dust and ashes" (Job 42:5–6). Finally Peter, after witnessing the miraculous power of the Messiah, fell to the feet of his Lord, "Go away from me Lord, for I am a sinful man!" (Luke 5:8). Even though we are approaching the holiness of the Lord in a different manner, the principle still rings true. The closer we get to His holiness, the more aware we become of our own sinfulness.

This doesn't appear to be at all pleasant. Who wants to their wretchedness brought to light? Nevertheless, it is a necessary step in charting our course and a natural product of the work of the Holy Spirit. Although we will become more cognizant of our corrupted nature, the Lord is drawing our attention to it in order to lead us in the way everlasting. Surely we can rejoice in the fact that these traits are being brought to light in order that they might be destroyed. We do well to remember that the same one who convicts us is also our Comforter.

If perfection doesn't come in this life, when does it actually occur? Our Father has fixed day when the redeemed all the ages will, in grand fashion, fulfill the commission of conformity to the image of Christ.

## THE CONSUMMATION OF THE QUEST

As previously noted, unlike the journeys of this world that often end in disappointment, our quest has a secure and sure consummation. As we chart our course, we must keep our eyes fixed on its finish line. This hope itself displays the purifying power already at work in our lives. As John proclaims:

> Beloved, now we are children of God, and it has not appeared as yet what we will be. We know that when He appears, we will be like Him, because we will see Him just as He is. And

> everyone who has this hope fixed on Him purifies
> himself, just as He is pure. (1 John 3:2–3)

It is when He appears that our journey will be complete. At that time, all the constituents of the kingdom of God will together be raised in immortality and carried to the Master. For "the Lord Himself will descend from heaven with a shout, with the voice of the archangel and with the trumpet of God, and the dead in Christ will rise first. Then we who are alive and remain will be caught up together with them in the clouds to meet the Lord in the air, and so we shall always be with the Lord" (1 Thess. 4:16–17).

When Christ appears, we will be clothed with our eternal immortal bodies and will enter into the fullness of our Master's joy. The purified pilgrims, upon the arrival at their eternal destination, will all sing the resurrection refrain:

> "Death is swallowed up in victory. O death,
> where is your victory? O death, where is your
> sting?" . . . The sting of death is sin, and the
> power of sin is the law; but thanks be to God,
> who gives us the victory through our Lord
> Jesus Christ. (1 Cor. 15–54–57)

This comprises our general course. The map is laid before us. As we progress on this path, our old self— the unredeemed child of Adam enslaved to sin and death—is being continually put to death. The flesh is being mortified. As this occurs, the new self, created in holiness, righteousness, and truth, is emerging. The Spirit is sanctifying.

The pilgrim's path is fraught with continuing conflict between our angelic foes, this ruthless world, and our old, ever-straying nature. As God's sure promise proclaims, the glorious fulfillment of this journey occurs when we are raised from the dead, when our lifeless flesh is transformed into immortality, and when not a speck of sin or drop of death exists in our being. *Death is swallowed up in victory.* Far from being wishful thinking, this is gospel truth.

## KNOW THY KING

While we do well to know our enemy and that which opposes us on our pilgrim's journey, the most important precept is to *know thy King.* Recall that the pilgrim's call is to shed all that hinders and "fix our eyes on Jesus, the author and finisher of our faith" (Heb. 12:3). We are continually to focus our attention and allegiance upon Jesus as He takes us from wretchedness to glory.

With this being *what* lies before us, we now must consider *how* are we called to accomplish it. What has God provided for us to continue on this path, and how are we, by His sustaining grace, to participate in this calling?

Before establishing the things with which we have been equipped to help us persevere on this journey, we must discern and avoid the pitfalls that mark our path.

---

[1] C. S. Lewis, *The Screwtape Letters* (New York: MacMillian, 1963), 3.

[2] We must take care not to push the imagery here too far. We do not have a split personality (even though sometimes it may feel like it). This is simply a way to describe the spiritual conflict that defines the believer's life. It highlights the two natures that reside

in the believer's being. The old self represents what we were in Adam. The new self represents what we are becoming in Christ. It is also necessary for us to avoid the temptation of using the old self as a way to avoid responsibility for sin. We are accountable and responsible for what arises out of our flesh if we choose to fulfill its desires. This all the more highlights our need to put on the new self.

[3] Owen, *Mortification*, 28.

[4] Jerry Bridges, *The Discipline of Grace* (Colorado Springs: NavPress, 1994), 196.

[5] J. C. Ryle, *Holiness* (Grand Rapids: Baker Book House, 1979), 27.

꿍

These are matters which have, to be sure, the appearance of wisdom in self-made religion and self-abasement and severe treatment of the body, but are of no value against fleshly indulgence.

Colossians 2:23

4

# Pitfalls Along the Path

*Avoiding Spiritual Snares that Line Our Way*

A little known biblical figure was given a monumental mission. A man named Tychius was entrusted by the apostle Paul with a scroll to deliver while Paul was locked in a Roman prison. Tychius' task was simple: Carry this urgent message to the church of Colossae. The enemy had set spiritual traps in the midst of those who were walking by the gospel of Jesus Christ. The peril was real, and these traps were set to take them captive. Paul penned indispensable wisdom to help the Colossians avoid these hindering snares. Little did Tychius know that he was bearing a message that would become essential for all whom God would place on the path of conformity to the image of Christ.

As we forge ahead through the harsh environments that constitute our course to the kingdom, we must be able to recognize the spiritual pitfalls. Outwardly, the traps may be adorned with enticements that promise quick advancement in our journey. Ultimately, however, they entangle us and hinder our ongoing quest. There is no shortage of offerings that promise to advance us on the path of righteousness. While pitfalls beset us on all sides, through the guiding power of God's Word, we are granted wisdom to navigate around them.

## RECOGNIZING THE SIGNS OF A SPIRITUAL PITFALL

By definition, pitfalls are hidden. They are dug under false ground and set up with a lure. When one treads upon the false ground, it gives way and the person is trapped. By their very nature, lures are intended to be enticing. Deception is at their heart. Hunters, trappers, and fisherman all seek to draw their prey near with elements that appear alluring but result in the demise of those who take the bait. Do not think that we are above such enticing. We have a roaring spiritual enemy seeking to devour us. Traps have been set up. Lures have been devised. We are the targets. The spiritual pitfalls that mark this world are too numerous to count. This makes recognizing and resisting them difficult. How do we identify these pitfalls so we can avoid them?

While the enemy has dug these obstacles, we are able to navigate around them by ascertaining their essence and understanding what they try to do. When the Lord inspired the apostle Paul to pen the epistle to the Colossians, the redeemed throughout the ages were granted an incomparable gift. In combating the false teaching that was prevalent at the time, the underlying essence of *all* spiritual pitfalls is revealed.

In its essence, the "Colossian heresy"[1] embodies the spiritual traps that have continued to appear on the spiritual landscape in different forms throughout the ages. In examining its elements, we behold the inspired guidance we need to recognize all teachings that "may have the appearance of wisdom but are of no value against the stopping of fleshly indulgence" (Col. 2:23). All such teaching has the appearance of being able to mortify our sinful impulses and advance us in being conformed to the image of Christ but in reality is deceptive, preventative, and destructive. It needs to be avoided.

## THE LURE OF SECRET KNOWLEDGE

The first alluring element of the Colossian heresy is the enticement of secret knowledge. There was an emphasis on the need to find and control the *stoichia*. Note Paul's concern as he establishes the only true foundation of spiritual growth:

> See to it that no one takes you captive through philosophy and empty deception, according to the tradition of men, according to the elementary principles [*stoichia*] of the world, rather than according to Christ. (Col. 2:8)

Notice the principles: philosophy, empty deception, the tradition of men, and the elementary principles of the world. These are lures designed to take us captive. In fact, the seduction of this teaching is so powerful that it has had offshoots throughout all history. It is especially prevalent today.

In order to control the elements around them, the false teachers in Colossae encouraged believers to find the *stoichia*. While many of the specifics are not known, what we do know is that Paul was combating a deceptive teaching encouraging the Colossians to control their fates through the discovery of elemental knowledge found in the unseen spiritual world. This teaching was seductive in that it promised spiritual advancement and control.[2] Paul forcefully responds by affirming the all-supremacy of Christ. There is no profit in seeking esoteric knowledge outside the realm of what has been revealed by God because Christ has overcome and secured us. There is no need to pursue anything but our unending relationship with Him. Regarding the triumph we share in the work of the Supreme Lord, we are taught:

> Let no one keep defrauding you of your prize by delighting in self-abasement and the worship of the angels, taking his stand on visions he has seen, inflated without cause by his fleshly mind, and not holding fast to the head, from whom the entire body, being supplied and held together by the joints and ligaments, grows with a growth which is from God. (Col. 2:18–19)

There is no need to consult any wisdom or philosophy that has not been granted through the commission of Christ. Whether its origins are in the minds of men or the mysterious realm of angelic magistrates, we are to avoid this lure and discern between what truly holds profit and what will result in ruin. Instead of chasing esoteric knowledge to combat our fallen natures, we are to hold fast to the Head, who has provided all the power and wisdom necessary for our sanctification.

This spiritual pitfall has numerous modern incarnations. There are hoards of teachings that encourage the believer to fix their focus on secret spiritual principles or the angelic realm. They postulate that in order to advance in the gospel and progress in sanctification, we must discover and overcome the evil spirits that are hindering progress. This is analogous to the teaching that Paul was rebuking. People were seeking the necessary wisdom and knowledge to control their fates through interacting with the spiritual realm.

To be sure, the spiritual realm is real. Precisely because it is real, it can also be very dangerous. Not only is seeking esoteric spiritual knowledge fruitless, but it is a fearful sphere to enter inappropriately. In the book of Jude, we read a sobering account of those who interacted with the spiritual realm in a prideful and disallowed manner:

> Yet in the same way these men, also by dreaming, defile the flesh, and reject authority, and revile angelic majesties. But Michael the archangel, when he disputed with the devil and argued about the body of Moses, did not dare pronounce against him a railing judgment, but said, "The Lord rebuke you!" (Jude 1:8–9)

There are indeed spiritual forces seeking us ruin. Rather than interacting inappropriately with the angelic realm, we need to realize the blessing we have in leaving these things to the King. He is all wise and all powerful. His might is supreme and His grace is sufficient. Trust Him to fight for us. Trust Him to sanctify us. Trust Him to work all things together for the good of those who love Him (Rom. 8:28).

Esoteric knowledge goes beyond the angelic realm. There are many who through their own imaginations and traditions teach either spiritual or secular principles that are raised up against the truth of Christ. Whether it be philosophical ponderings or the practice of finding and controlling inner psychological phenomena, all of these lead to ruin as they cause us to not hold fast to the Head. Rather than being taken captive by these seductive teachings, we are commanded to take all these thoughts captive for the King.

> For though we walk in the flesh, we do not war according to the flesh, for the weapons of our warfare are not of the flesh, but divinely powerful for the destruction of fortresses. We are destroying speculations and every lofty thing raised up against the knowledge of God, and we are taking every thought captive to the obedience of Christ. (2 Cor. 10:3–5)

There is certainly no shortage of human wisdom that "raises itself up" against the knowledge of Christ. Through the divinely powerful weapons granted to us in Christ, it is our duty to recognize them, whether without or within, and thwart their effort to take us captive with their enticing lures.

Those who offer these "secret" truths are the spiritual equivalents of con artists. They are superficial and self-serving. We do well to recognize their folly. We are not commissioned to discover secret, esoteric knowledge. Rather we are called to ignore and avoid it because in Christ we are complete. His supremacy has granted us the knowledge and wisdom that is sufficient for our quest to be conformed to His image. It is all the wisdom and knowledge we need.

## THE LURE OF LEGALISM

Another alluring element of the Colossian heresy was, in order to accomplish the control of the "fates" by discovering this secret knowledge, certain rites and observances were necessary. Observance of the Mosaic code was evident in the Colossian heresy because Paul speaks of circumcision, food laws, Sabbaths, and other aspects of the Jewish calendar.

> [I]n Him you were also circumcised with a circumcision made without hands, in the removal of the body of the flesh by the circumcision of Christ . . . Therefore let no one act as your judge in regard to food or drink or in respect to a festival or a new moon or a Sabbath day—things which are a mere shadow of what is to come; but the substance belongs to Christ. (Col. 2:14–16)

Among the Colossians, there was a clear emphasis on observing the Mosaic Law and its stipulations in order to advance in the conquest of their fleshly desires. However, we must understand that these observances, although necessary at their intended time, were shadows of the Savior. The prescribed sacrifices under the Old Covenant are no longer in operation because that to which they pointed was accomplished. The ultimate sacrifice has been made, and the perfect Priest has eternally atoned (Heb. 9:11–12). The observance of Sabbath is not binding because Jesus has come and granted us the rest that the Sabbath signified (Heb. 4:3, Col. 2:16). It is not necessary to undergo circumcision as a sign of being a child of Abraham. Rather, it is a circumcised heart through the work of Christ that makes one a child of Abraham (Gal. 5:2–4, Col. 2:11). The supremacy of Christ and the sufficiency of His work is the issue. Since true purifying power is in the finished work of the Son, it is fruitless and dishonoring to the King to demand a return to the shadows since He has commanded us to leave these practices behind.

Those who encourage and necessitate a return to the elements of the Old Covenant are continuing this entangling work. As constituents of the New Covenant community, it has been divinely decreed that we are no longer under the yoke of the Old Covenant.[3] In light of the coming Christ, if it is perilous to return to the practices that at one time were a necessary work of obedience for the Covenant community, how much more does this ring true for practices that never had the seal of the Lord upon them to begin with? We must be alert and avoid the lure of legalism.

## THE LURE OF ASCETICISM

Coupled with the legalistic regimen, there was an ascetic undertone to this false teaching. Asceticism is the harsh treatment of the physical body in an attempt to attain spiritual life. It is often accompanied by a withdrawal from society in an attempt to flee the temptations of the world. Paul notes this element in writing:

> If you have died with Christ to the elementary principles of the world, why, as if you were living in the world, do you submit yourself to decrees, such as, "Do not handle, do not taste, do not touch!" (which all refer to things destined to perish with the using)—in accordance with the commandments and teachings of men? (Col. 2:20–22)

Paul continues to note that this spiritual pitfall also entailed the severe treatment of the body. In order to attempt to curtail the lusts of the flesh, an ascetic life was the proposed solution.

It is indeed true that we are not "in this world" in one sense. If we are in Christ, we are told regarding the accomplished plan of the Father: "He rescued us from the domain of darkness, and transferred us to the kingdom of His beloved Son" (Col. 1:13). But this does not prescribe withdrawing from society as the manner to escape and conquer the desires of the flesh. Rather, the opposite is true. History is wrought with examples of those who withdrew from society and practiced severe treatment of the body only to find themselves further oppressed by the desires of the flesh.

Prior to his awakening to the all supremacy and sufficiency of Jesus Christ, the reformer Martin Luther lived a life of asceticism. As a monk devoted to isolation, he did not discover a tranquil life free of temptation. On the contrary, he became haunted by the deceitful desires of the wicked human heart. He became so distraught with his sinfulness in light of the holiness of God that he would scourge himself to attempt to curtail the enemy within. There are even more radical examples. There is an account of a man by the name of Simon Stylites who became so distraught over the influx of people near his selected cave that he perched himself on top of a pole for thirty years in an attempt to withdraw. The real saints were those who picked up after him all that time.

We may not behold the practice of asceticism to this degree, but asceticism still has a pervasive presence today. A life of isolation and rigorous

65

treatment of the body has the appearance of self-denial, and many in the church advance this as a necessary means of sanctification. Like the other lures, this is simply a deceptive means that has no power to produce godliness.

## NECESSARY NAVIGATION

Given the essence of the false teaching evident in Paul's exhortation to the Colossians, and given the numerous offshoots that are implicated, let us move forward with these principles firmly set in our spiritual vision. A clarified worldview will help us avoid these pitfalls when they attempt to take us captive. To repeat the authoritative apostolic verdict:

> These are matters which have, to be sure, the appearance of wisdom in self-made religion and self-abasement and severe treatment of the body, but are of no value against fleshly indulgence. (Col. 2:23)

There are thousands of variations to these pitfalls, so we must recognize their essence in order to avoid becoming ensnared by their offshoots. Indeed, there is a common underlying deception in all man-made religion; it denies the supremacy and sufficiency of Christ. It undermines the gospel by taking our eyes off the person and finished work of Jesus on the cross.

> For in Him all the fullness of Deity dwells in bodily form, and in Him you have been made complete, and He is the head over all rule and authority. (Col. 2:9–10)

The supremacy and sufficiency of Jesus Christ is not dry, dusty doctrine. It is the practical, eternal truth that saturates our souls. Fixing our eyes upon Him and His supremacy not only frees us from man-made religion, it enables us to avoid the traps that have as their very purpose to distract us from this endeavor.

If you have slipped into one of these spiritual pitfalls, consider this your calling to climb out. Your sovereign Shepherd is able to draw you out of the pit and place you back on the straight and narrow path. Dispense of these useless practices and return to the simplicity of faith in the finished work of Jesus Christ. Through His renewing grace, you will be able to re-establish a fruitful walk within His merciful boundaries.

## AVOIDING THE PITFALLS: THE COMMON DENOMINATOR

In light of all these truths, the underlying deception of spiritual pitfalls is this:

*The common denominator of all spiritual pitfalls is pursuing that which is not centered on the person and finished work of Jesus Christ and continuing in ways that are not granted by divine authority.*

You have what you need in Him and in His accomplished redemptive work. He is the head over all rule and authority. He is wisest of the wise. He is the way, the truth, and the life. Our salvation is a completed task, and our Lord is the all-sufficient reservoir for our spiritual needs. Why focus upon the spiritual world of angels and demons when He is above them? Why consult human wisdom when He is infinitely wiser and has granted us His sufficient counsel? Why center on rituals when His purifying power is the only authentic source that has any value against fleshly indulgence? Content in His supremacy and His sufficiency, we will forge ahead, avoiding these perilous traps and fixing our eyes on the author and finisher of our faith.

With divinely bestowed clarity regarding what needs to be avoided, we naturally must then ask: What has the Lord granted us to proceed? Since we are made complete in Him, what then has our King commanded that we devote ourselves to in order continue the quest? Let us behold the divinely inspired answer to what must we do to proceed on the path of conformity to the image of Christ.

---

[1] There are various theories on the precise nature of the Colossian heresy. While we cannot nail down with certainty its exact elements, its effects and general nature are revealed through a careful reading of the text. One recent work that incorporates recent archaeological evidence that may illuminate some of the specifics is Clinton E. Arnold's *The Colossian Syncretism—The Interface between Christianity and Folk Belief at Colossae* (Baker: Grand Rapids, 1996).

[2] Secret knowledge is that which God has chosen not to reveal. Because this knowledge resides not in the realm of either general revelation (creation) or specific revelation (the Scriptures), it is not permissible for us to pursue.

[3] The account that best highlights this decree is Acts 15, which is known as the Jerusalem Council. The Judaizing heresy has its elements in the Colossian heresy, is prominent in Galatians, and is the issue that prompts the Jerusalem Council. The issue of whether or not Gentiles are required to obey the Mosaic Law and its stipulations (e.g. Sabbath, food laws, circumcision) was the driving force behind this council. The apostles came to agreement and did not bind the disciples of Christ to the Mosaic Law but rather loosed them from it. Requiring a return to these elements,

as further demonstrated in Galatians and Hebrews, is not only unnecessary but disobedient to the faith delivered once for all.

❧❧

But I say, walk by the Spirit, and you will not carry out the desire of the flesh.

Galatians 5:16

5

# Walking by the Spirit

*Discerning What We Are Called to Do*

How are we called to walk as believers in the King? As previously noted, in the initial days of my walk, once I ascertained the call for conformity to the image of Christ, I was confronted with the painful reality of the struggle with sin. As I proceeded along this path, I found myself falling into the pitfalls that I have just outlined. A legalistic regimen did nothing to curtail the works of sin. An ascetic lifestyle created more problems than it solved. The search for secret, esoteric knowledge hindered spiritual progress rather than producing advancement towards the goal of sanctification. I vividly recall the despair that such a state produces. Yet, in the midst of the darkness, the light of God's Word pierced through, offering the divinely bestowed answer to what we are called to do in our quest, and more specifically, by *whom* we are called to walk.

In my Scriptural endeavors, I came upon a foundational text in the book of Galatians. The teaching of this text illuminates the path in which all of God's pilgrims need to engage in order to avoid the

71

perilous traps lining our way. In the midst of Paul's contention for the purity of the one true faith, he gives this command:

> But I say, *walk by the Spirit*, and you will not carry out the desire of the flesh. For the flesh sets its desire against the Spirit, and the Spirit against the flesh; for these are in opposition to one another, so that you may not do the things that you please. (Gal. 5:16–18, emphasis mine)

In this God-breathed exhortation, a couple of principles were clearly evident to me. First, this text reflected the conflict that was expressing itself in my life. There was an intense struggle between the flesh and the Spirit. The Spirit had brought renewal and desire for holiness in the Lord, yet the flesh opposed this holiness, seeking to entice and entangle. Beyond this, a clear, concise command captured my attention. There was an exhortation as to what I needed to do in order to not fulfill the desires of the flesh. My marching orders were to *walk by the Spirit*. Since this is such a significant text in our quest for sanctification, let us carefully consider what this command actually means, both in its essence and in its surrounding context.

## THE GALATIAN SITUATION

When one reads the opening of Paul's polemic in the book of Galatians, we are introduced to a rather fiery apostle. Rather than his typical greeting of thanksgiving, Paul opens with a curse.

> I am amazed that you are so quickly deserting Him who called you by the grace of Christ, for a different gospel; which is really not another;

only there are some who are disturbing you and want to distort the gospel of Christ. But even if we, or an angel from heaven, should preach to you a gospel contrary to what we have preached to you, he is to be accursed! As we have said before, so I say again now, if any man is preaching to you a gospel contrary to what you received, he is to be accursed! (Gal. 1:6–9)

What was it that caused Paul to use such strong language? What situation had arisen in Galatia that drew this ire? A group that history has labeled the Judaizers had infiltrated this particular church and, as the rest of the New Testament corpus reveals, their teachings were widespread throughout the early incarnation of the church.

Jesus of Nazareth ushered in a new era of salvation history. Because of the coming of the Messiah and His accomplished work, the Lord instituted the New Covenant. In light of the new, the old had passed away. Therefore, the covenant that was instituted at Sinai had passed away, and now the faithful community of the redeemed lived through the tenets of the New Covenant instituted by Christ and proclaimed by His apostles.

Not surprisingly, this caused contention with the Jewish populous that rejected the claims of Christ. Imagine the shock that such a radical change brought to a culture that had continued in these traditions for thousands of years. Nevertheless, the sacrificial system, the dietary laws, Sabbath observance, the Jewish calendar, circumcision, and other elements of the ceremonial law had found their fulfillment in the person and redemptive work of the Messiah.

73

In this climate, a sect had arisen that declared that while Jesus was indeed the Messiah, the Gentiles must still observe the Law of Moses in addition to placing their faith in Christ. This is what Paul declared to be a different gospel. Why was this teaching such a serious departure that it drew Paul's curse? Because it implicitly denied the power and finished work of Jesus Christ. By mandating the elements of the Old Covenant, one was publicly denying that the New Covenant was in effect and thus dishonored the work of redemption accomplished by our King.

Paul's response to the Judaizing heresy was a proclamation of salvation by grace through faith alone. His rhetoric is unmistakable: "This is the only thing I want to find out from you: did you receive the Spirit by the works of the Law, or by hearing with faith? Are you so foolish? Having begun by the Spirit, are you now being perfected by the flesh?" (Gal. 5:2–3). Paul was not completely dismissing the role of the Law in the life of the believer,[1] but he was establishing that we are saved and sanctified by grace through faith in the person and finished work of Jesus Christ. We have received the Spirit, signaling the dawn of a new era.

Since we are not called to observe the Mosaic Law, the question arises: How are we to live under this New Covenant established by our King? How are we to embark upon our journey? With the inauguration of the New Covenant, a radical new way of life was established. The commissioned children are not to live in either extreme of legalism or unbridled liberty. Rather, they are to live by the Spirit of the living God. In order to proceed on the path of purification, we must walk by the Spirit.

## THE COMMAND AND THE PROMISE

"Walk by the Spirit and you will not fulfill the desires of the flesh." This rich exhortation is begun by a command and concluded with a promise. Paul commands his faithful readers to "walk." The Greek word that Paul utilizes here (*peripate*) is used to denote how one carries out his everyday living. In utilizing this word, Paul is cultivating a concept not only of how one lives but also how one progresses.

This lifestyle is by the Spirit. The Greek word utilized here for "Spirit" is *pneumna*. While this word carries a broad range of meaning, the context is clear: Paul is referring to the Holy Spirit. Recalling the context of the book of Galatians, Paul is struggling against the precept that a believer in the person and work of Christ must continue in the prescripted laws given by God to Moses. The ceremonial commands given at Sinai were to be obeyed until the one to whom they pointed arrived and fulfilled their intentions. Now that the Law has been fulfilled in Christ, we do not seek to live or walk according to its prescriptions. Instead, Christ has sent the Comforter to accomplish His righteousness in our lives. Therefore, we must live according to the power and prescriptions of the Spirit, not according to Sinai.

If we heed the command to walk by the Spirit or "live by the power and prescriptions of the Holy Spirit," who is applying Christ's righteousness to our lives, we "will not carry out the desires of the flesh." The phrase "carry out" can also be translated "fulfill" or "gratify." In light of this, the underlying principle is the practice of "cutting off" the process that leads to sin. If you walk by the Spirit, you will not bring to fruition the deeds of the flesh.

Just what is the flesh (Gr. *sarx*)? Like the word "spirit" (Gr. *pnuema*), this word contains a wide range of meaning. Given the context and its consistent use in the letters of Paul, the flesh here refers to the fallen nature of the old self, the residues of the pollution that resides in our unredeemed state. We may be tempted to associate the flesh only with the sins of the body (such as lust, drunkenness, and other physical passions), but as will be made manifest in the context of this command, the flesh also consists of sins beyond this realm. Therefore, the term here denotes the entire fallen personal domain from which all sin and impurity sprouts.

The apostle James proclaims this perilous portion of our personhood. In his epistle, he describes the deceptive desires that bring forth dastardly consequences.

> Let no one say when he is tempted, "I am being tempted by God"; for God cannot be tempted by evil, and He Himself does not tempt anyone. But each one is tempted when he is carried away and enticed by his own lust. Then when lust has conceived, it gives birth to sin; and when sin is accomplished, it brings forth death. (James 1:13–15)

James grants us insight into the progression of sin. It begins with our own lust, our own fallen nature that sprouts its sinful impulses. These desires are brought forth and, once birthed, result in death. In order to abort this destructive process, we are commanded to live our lives by the Spirit. By the Spirit's grace, we will conquer the sinful desires that so easily entangle us and, in turn, cultivate the fruit of the Spirit.

These truths are presented by Paul in Romans 8. He writes:

> So then, brethren, we are under obligation, not to the flesh, to live according to the flesh—for if you are living according to the flesh, you must die; but if *by the Spirit* you are putting to death the deeds of the body, you will live. (Rom. 8:12–13, emphasis mine)

Thus, as we walk by the Spirit, we experience a life of ever-increasing righteousness and ever-decreasing sin. In short, sanctification is produced when one proceeds to "walk by the Spirit." Just what does this life look like? Paul proceeds to note what we must conquer and what we must cultivate in this divine quest.

## THAT WHICH WE MUST CONQUER

Since the flesh is the source from which ungodly desires sprout, Paul gives us a rather extensive list of the evil deeds that result when the desires of the flesh are fulfilled. In a very real sense, this is a list of our targeted enemies. We must recognize their reality and set our attitudes against them.

> Now the deeds of the flesh are evident, which are: immorality, impurity, sensuality, idolatry, sorcery, enmities, strife, jealousy, outbursts of anger, disputes, dissensions, factions, envying, drunkenness, carousing, and things like these, of which I forewarn you, just as I have forewarned you, that those who practice such

things will not inherit the kingdom of God.
(Gal. 5:19–21)

This, of course, is not an exhaustive list but rather a dynamic one that outlines the various types of deeds that lead to death. The list begins with sexual sins: immorality, impurity, and sensuality. These three express the various misuses of God's gifts. "Immorality" is the practice of sex outside of God's institution of marriage, while "impurity" is the state resulting from such. This illustrious list continues with an assortment of relational sins: enmities, strife, jealousy, outbursts of anger, dissentions, factions, envying. These various behaviors all have discourse and pride at their root. "Drunkenness" and "carousing" are the misuse of alcohol and its resulting destructive behaviors. Paul concludes the list with "and things like these." There are others: partiality, favoritism, pride, and the list could continue *ad nauseum.*

We are then given a sobering warning which all the more highlights our need to conquer these treacherous traits: "I forewarn you, just as I have forewarned you, that those who practice such things will not inherit the kingdom of God." Was Paul now resorting to salvation by works? If we trip up and sin in one of these ways, is our eternal inheritance revoked? Certainly not, as Paul has just completed a powerful proclamation of salvation by grace through faith alone. Just what then is meant here and how does it apply?

Paul uses the word *prasso* to describe the action (practice) leading to the perilous result (no inheritance of the kingdom of God). This is descriptive of a continuous, ongoing, unrepentant way of life. It is basically in stark contrast to those who walk by the Spirit. Those who walk by the Spirit by definition cannot continue in this way in the sense of unhindered practice of these sins. The presence and work of the Holy Spirit causes our conflict with these perilous practices. Therefore, Paul is not speaking of a "trip up" here, but rather an unhindered, unrepentant lifestyle. If this is the case, the Spirit is absent and therefore there is no inheritance awaiting those who walk in such a manner. With this being the case, this places a spotlight on the command to conquer the things of the flesh. It is part and parcel to our new nature and call to wage war against such things, demonstrating our spiritual position and guiding us forward toward cultivating the characteristics of those who are destined to inherit the kingdom of God.

## THAT WHICH WE MUST CULTIVATE

While the fulfilling of the desires of the flesh results in death and corruption, cultivating the fruit of the Spirit results in life and conformity to the image of Christ. We are given a list of the bountiful life that results from walking by the Spirit.

> But the fruit of the Spirit is love, joy, peace, patience, kindness, goodness, faithfulness, gentleness, self-control; against such things there is no law. (Gal. 5:22–23)

With the work of the Holy Spirit having tilled the ground of our hearts, we have a dynamic list of what our lives should (and indeed will) look like as we walk by the Spirit of the living God. We are granted "three sets of three" describing the transformation of our

79

attitudes and character: *love*, *joy*, and *peace* are divine characteristics that spring forth through our understanding and realization of God's grace in Christ. *Patience*, *kindness*, and *goodness* describe the outworking of our lives with others, being in stark contrast to the relational traits of the flesh. Finally, *faithfulness*, *gentleness*, and *self-control* speak of our developing, enduring mastery over unbelief, pride, and their deathly offshoots, the works of the flesh.

All of these characteristics are overarching descriptions of the bountiful, lasting fruit that God has planted His Holy Spirit in our lives to produce.

## The Living Way

With the corruptive deeds of the flesh noted and the sprouting fruit of the Spirit described, we are granted a final, resolute call to march forth in the Sprit's prescribed manner.

> Now those who belong to Christ Jesus have crucified the flesh with its passions and desires. If we live by the Spirit, let us also walk by the Spirit. (Gal. 5:25)

A very important point is established here that one must be careful not to miss. If we have believed, then we have the Spirit of God. If we have the Spirit of God, then we are Christ's possession. We are His people. Since we are His people, it is the cross that has destroyed the work of the flesh. The crucifixion was where our flesh—the unbelieving, sinful child of Adam—was put to death. The Spirit is now applying the work of the cross to our lives. We are spiritually alive because of the Spirit. We must continue by keeping in step with Him. Therefore, the call goes forward: Those who are have been given life by the Spirit must continue to walk by the Spirit.

The flesh is conquered. It is an already defeated foe. Our sanctification is a completed task by Christ on the cross. We must recognize this so we do not fall into the pitfall of legalistic works. He accomplished the totality of our redemption once for all. It is accomplished. This is why Paul can proclaim that "the flesh *has been* crucified"—past tense. Sin was dealt with at the cross. Christ's righteousness is now our righteousness. We are justified once for all through faith because of the cross. Now, through the continuing grace of the risen Lord, His accomplished work is being applied through our journey. We are not earning this sanctification but rather, as we walk by the Spirit, His righteousness is graciously being applied to our lives.

## THE UNANSWERED QUESTION

At this point, there may be a question nagging at you. This text is very clear about *what* we must do. We are called to walk by the Spirit. However, your response may be, as mine was, "Yes, I long to walk by the Spirit of the living God, *how* am I to accomplish it?" Although the command is clear, the text is vague in how we are to accomplish it. Paul does not clearly outline the specific principles. This does not mean we are left to guess or that the Scriptures are silent on this issue. When we explore the whole counsel of God, we begin to understand those things that accomplish this command. While they are gifts, they carry accountability. John Owen well appraises us regarding our responsibility:

> Not to be daily employing the Spirit and new nature for the mortifying of sin, is to neglect that excellent succour which God has given us against our greatest enemy. If we neglect to make use of what we have received, God may justly hold his hand from giving us more. His graces as well as his gifts are given and bestowed on us to use, exercise and trade with. Not to be daily mortifying sin is to sin against the goodness, kindness, wisdom, grace and love of God, who has furnished us with a principle of doing it.[2]

God has provided His Spirit and His Spirit-filled means to accomplish the destruction of sin and produce the unveiling of the new self. We are commanded to participate. Therefore, let us proceed to explore, and heed, precisely how we are called to walk by the Spirit.

---

[1] A careful reading of both Galatians and Romans will reveal that that God's moral commands are still binding in this age. While the ceremonial law found its fulfillment in Christ, the moral law of God both reveals God's righteousness and reveals our sin. It also provides guidance for how we are to live. The Law, though completely fulfilled in Christ, is still upheld by the Christian when properly defined.

[2] Owen, *Mortification*, 34.

They were continually devoting themselves to the apostles' teaching and to fellowship, to the breaking of bread and to prayer.

Acts 2:42

6

# The Simple Truth

*The Divine Answer to How We Walk by the Spirit*

C reation had waited with baited breath for this very moment. It had endured the curse and the purging of the flood and witnessed the promise of renewal. Then, through the execution of the Christ outside the city of Jerusalem, the cosmos was reconciled (Col. 1:19–20). The promise that had its inception in centuries past began to unfold.

The day of Pentecost, following the Passover of Christ, served as the first breath of the new life that will continue to spread until the renewing work of the Holy Spirit is fulfilled. Throughout the centuries, the Spirit has continued to gather and purify the constituents of the kingdom; and as constituents, we draw ever closer to the consummation. "For the anxious longing of the creation waits eagerly for the revealing of the sons of God" (Rom. 8:19). While the sons won't be fully revealed until the consummation, the initial sign of the outpouring of the Spirit signaled that renewal has begun.

## THE OUTPOURING

The Lord told of this glorious event weeks prior to His Pentecost: "When the Helper comes, whom I will send to you from the Father, that is the Spirit of truth who proceeds from the Father, He will testify about Me" (John 15:26). Jesus further explained: "But I tell you the truth, it is to your advantage that I go away; for if I do not go away, the Helper will not come to you; but if I go, I will send Him to you." In the Greek, the term translated "helper" here is *paraclete*, which can also carry the connotation of "advocate" and "comforter."

How could it be more beneficial for the Lord to leave and send the Holy Spirit? For the believer, it is because He comes to regenerate, reveal, and renew. When confronted regarding the miraculous signs that accompanied the initial outpouring of the Spirit, Peter stood and proclaimed:

> "Men of Judea and all you who live in Jerusalem, let this be known to you and give heed to my words. For these men are not drunk, as you suppose, for it is only the third hour of the day; but this is what was spoken of through the prophet Joel: 'And it shall be in the last days,' God says, 'That I will pour forth of My Spirit on all mankind; and your sons and your daughters shall prophesy, and your young men shall see visions, and your old men shall dream dreams; even on My bondslaves, both men and women, I will in those days pour forth of My Spirit and they shall prophesy. (Acts 2:14–18)

Simon Peter, who had cowered at the prospect of suffering for Christ just weeks earlier, now proceeded to powerfully announce the arrival of the New Covenant and the kingdom of God in the person and work of Jesus Christ. In his Pentecost address, he called those listening to partake in the New Covenant by repenting and believing in Jesus Christ, the risen King.

> "Therefore let all the house of Israel know for certain that God has made Him both Lord and Christ—this Jesus whom you crucified." Now when they heard this, they were pierced to the heart, and said to Peter and the rest of the apostles, "Brethren, what shall we do?" Peter said to them, "Repent, and each of you be baptized in the name of Jesus Christ for the forgiveness of your sins; and you will receive the gift of the Holy Spirit. For the promise is for you and your children and for all who are far off, as many as the Lord our God will call to Himself." (Acts 2:36–39)

So the outpouring had begun. The promise of the Holy Spirit was upon them. The renewing power of God was being applied in a radical new way. The old had passed away and the new had arrived. This promise was even for "all who are far off, as many as the Lord our God will call to Himself" (Acts 2:39).

Now that the Spirit had been poured out, how was this new community under the kingship of Christ supposed to live? How were those who repented and believed the message of Jesus Christ called to continue in this power from on high? In other words, how were they to walk by the Spirit?

## How We Walk by the Spirit

It started with baptism. The New Covenant community was being established, and initiation into this community was through the rite of baptism. Luke continues to chronicle this account by noting: "So then, those who had received his word were baptized" (Acts 2:41). Baptism was a significant sign for two reasons. It was both a public identification with the person and work of Jesus Christ and a personal proclamation of being under the New Covenant.

Those who came through the waters into a new way of living were no longer under the Old Covenant. Rather, they had experienced the initial outpouring of God's fulfilled promise. Thus, Luke chronicles the way this radical new community walked:

> They were continually devoting themselves to the apostles' teaching and to fellowship, to the breaking of bread and to prayer. (Acts 2:42)

Here in this simple, straightforward description resides a renewing truth that defines the New Covenant community. They heard the gospel, they believed the gospel, and now they were continuing in how God wanted them to proceed in the gospel. In this passage, we receive the prescription for how we are to walk by the Spirit. The opening verb that is used to describe their activity is *proskartereo*, "continually devoted." This is the same concept conveyed by the word "walk" in Galatians 5:16. It is a lifestyle, a perpetual endeavor, an ongoing process.

There were three central aspects to this spiritually inaugurated walk.

The first was devotion to the apostles' teaching. Since this point is foundational for all that follows, it is imperative that we understand its significance. The apostles' teaching was the fulfillment of Christ's instruction to them: "Go therefore and make disciples of all the nations, baptizing them in the name of the Father and the Son and the Holy Spirit, teaching them to observe all that I commanded you" (Matt. 28:19–20). The apostles were not teaching something conjured up in their own minds but rather announcing the divinely instituted precepts of the New Covenant established by Jesus Christ. So their devotion was to the Word of God, specifically to the Word of God in light of the fulfillment of the promise in Jesus of Nazareth.

Secondly, they devoted themselves to prayer. Prayer has always been a mark of the faithful community of God. But in wake of the finished work of Christ and the inauguration of the Spirit, prayer took on a radical new dynamic. The Lord sent His Son to die so that He would be raised as our eternal Intercessor. Through the work of the Spirit, we now approach the throne of grace with our eternal salvation as a completed task. The New Covenant community approaches the Father with its High Priest as a forerunner who has revolutionized our relationship and communication with God forever.

Finally, they devoted themselves to fellowship and the breaking of bread.[1] Since Jesus had made the perfect sacrifice, all foreshadows of temple worship found their ultimate fulfillment in Him. The temple and its administrators were no longer the center of worship. Rather, what Jesus had told the Samaritan woman had come to fruition:

89

> Jesus said to her, "Woman, believe Me, an hour
> is coming when neither in this mountain nor in
> Jerusalem will you worship the Father. You
> worship what you do not know; we worship
> what we know, for salvation is from the Jews.
> But an hour is coming, and now is, when the
> true worshipers will worship the Father in spirit
> and truth; for such people the Father seeks to be
> His worshipers. (John 4:21–23)

That hour came with the first coming of Christ. It
came to a crescendo at Pentecost and continues to this
day. The New Testament affirms that a new era has
dawned, and now the Holy Spirit powerfully dwells
through the fellowship of believers in Jesus Christ.
The members of the early New Covenant community
devoted themselves to this radical new way of worship.
Through gathering together, they no longer offered
the blood sacrifices but "the breaking of bread." In
this act of worship, they both remembered the perfect
sacrifice and looked forward to the feast that awaits all
who walk by the Spirit. As fellow pilgrims with the
initial partakers of the Spirit of God, we are exhorted
to do likewise. We are to continually devote ourselves
to the Word of God, to prayer, to fellowship, and to
the breaking of bread. In doing so, with faith as our
fuel, we will be walking by the Spirit.

## PRESCRIPTIVE OR SIMPLY DESCRIPTIVE?

Some may object to this, stating: "This text is simply
describing what the church did at Pentecost. It is not
necessarily prescribing what we all should do." This is
a valid observation, but I think the text is compellingly
clear in presenting these as both descriptive and

prescriptive.[2] If these are God's chosen means to purify His people, we would expect to find confirming evidence in other portions of Scripture. Indeed, we do. Two other extremely important biblical contexts confirm this as the lifestyle in which all the redeemed are to engage.[3]

## THE COLOSSIANS CONFIRMATION

As previously established, Paul's epistle to the Colossians was a reaffirmation of the supremacy and sufficiency of Jesus Christ in the face of false teaching. The teachings that Paul combated sought to ensnare the disciples of Christ into a lifestyle that was far removed from that to which they had been called. The search for esoteric knowledge, a legalistic regimen, and an ascetic lifestyle were the wrong way to pursue purity. After establishing the unending sufficiency of Jesus' finished work, the apostle announced that such false means of sanctification "have the appearance of wisdom but are of no value against fleshly indulgence" (2:23). So what *is* of value against the flesh? What *is* the way to put to death the old self and put on the new (Col. 3:10–12)? The apostle proceeds to give us a familiar framework.

First, we are exhorted to "Let the word of Christ richly dwell within you, with all wisdom teaching and admonishing one another with psalms and hymns and spiritual songs, singing with thankfulness in your hearts to God" (Col. 3:16). The Word of God as delivered through Christ and His apostles is to *dwell richly* in us as we pursue this goal. Furthering this continuing quest, we must *"put on love,* which is the perfect bond of unity. Let the peace of Christ rule in your hearts, to which indeed you were called in one body; and be thankful" (Col. 3:14–15, emphasis mine). The bond of fellowship must be kept in this ongoing operation of the soul.

Finally, in our journey to being conformed the image of Jesus, we are plainly exhorted: "Devote yourselves to *prayer*, keeping alert in it with an attitude of thanksgiving" (Col. 4:2, emphasis mine).

Therefore, through the inspiration of the Holy Spirit, the apostle Paul has exhorted those under the all-sufficient banner of Jesus' supremacy to be continually devoted to the Word of God, to fellowship, and to prayer. In the midst of this exhortation, he makes it clear we are to be thankful because we have been granted all we need in our Lord. He exhorts us to walk the one way of sanctification. He exhorts us to walk by the Spirit.

## THE HEBREWS CONFIRMATION

In Hebrews, the context of the book has a corresponding link to the context of Colossians. Like Paul, the mysterious author of Hebrews is concerned that his readers continue in the supremacy of Christ and His completed work on Calvary. As one proceeds through Hebrews, it is apparent that the author is establishing that Jesus is greater than all that was held dear under the Old Covenant. Jesus is greater than the angels, greater than Moses, greater than the temple, greater than Aaron, and greater than the Levitical sacrificial system. In short, He is greater than all. Therefore, it is imperative that the community under the New Covenant remain in His finished work and not return to the shadows of the Old Covenant.

Since the New Covenant community of God is not to return to the temple rites, nor to the old priestly sacrificial system, nor to any of the elements that have found their substance in Christ, how does the writer of Hebrews command His readers to continue?

The author clearly establishes the need to engage in devotion to the Word of God. In fact, the author is distressed that those with whom he is acquainted have remained in a state of infancy in their interaction with the Word. He addresses those whom he has diagnosed with this shortcoming, admonishing them:

> For everyone who partakes only of milk is not accustomed to the word of righteousness, for he is an infant. But solid food is for the mature, who because of practice have their senses trained to discern good and evil. Therefore leaving the elementary teaching about the Christ, let us *press on to maturity*. (Heb. 5:15–6:1, emphasis mine)

Devotion to the Word of God is essential to those being conformed into the righteous image of Christ.

In light of the coming of Christ, the author also impresses upon his readers that we need not go to any earthly throne. We must approach the throne of heaven through the endeavor of prayer.

> Therefore let us *draw near with confidence to the throne of grace*, so that we may receive mercy and find grace to help in time of need. (Heb. 4:16, emphasis mine)

We are commanded to engage in prayer—to draw near the throne of grace—in order to receive mercy and grace. It is through this endeavor that God grants us His power to overcome and to walk the path of sanctification and spiritual growth.

Finally, we are commanded not to cast off the gathering together of believers. Rather, we are to devote ourselves to the blessings of fellowship.

> Let us hold fast the confession of our hope without wavering, for He who promised is faithful; and let us consider how to stimulate one another to love and good deeds, *not forsaking our own assembling together*, as is the habit of some, but encouraging one another; and all the more as you see the day drawing near. (Heb. 23–25, emphasis mine)

The elements of the Old Covenant pointed to Jesus. Now He has arrived and accomplished. Therefore, there has been great change in how and where we meet God. No longer do we need to engage in the sacrificial system. We have a great High Priest, Jesus, who has gone through the heavens, and we now may approach God through the radical new endeavor of prayer through Him. No longer do God's chosen people need to gather in Jerusalem at the temple because His Spirit dwells in their collective hearts through faith. No longer do we need to be under a chosen prophet to grant us guidance because God's Son has arrived and delivered His sufficient word once for all. Therefore, we must continue in what God has revealed. We must walk the path of God's chosen means. Only then will we progress in conformity to the image of Christ.

## THE "SPIRITUAL" ENDEAVORS

As seen in the events at the beginning of Acts, these endeavors are by no means new. They have been the prescribed foundation for walking by the Spirit since the day the Spirit was poured out. They have marked the history of the Church and not changed from the initial outpouring of the Holy Spirit to His continuing work today. In his classic work, *Holiness*, J. C. Ryle well explains the Spirit's means of sanctification.

> Sanctification, again, is a thing which depends greatly on a diligent use of Scriptural means. When I speak of "means" I have in view Bible-reading, private prayer, regular attendance of public worship, regular hearing of God's word, and regular reception of the Lord's Supper. I lay it down as a simple matter of fact, that no one who is careless about such things must ever expect to make much progress in sanctification. I can find no record of any eminent saint who ever neglected them. They are appointed channels through which the Holy Spirit conveys fresh supplies of grace to the soul and strengthens the work which He has begun in the inward man.[4]

Lest we miss the significance of how these endeavors are indeed the means the Spirit Himself has established, allow me to outline exactly how the Holy Spirit is intensely active in their proper use.

The Spirit has an inseparable connection to the Scriptures. Not only has He moved the mouths of the prophets and guided the pens of the writers, He grants the believer illumination regarding the value and significance of His truth, driving His life-changing precepts into the human heart. Paul notes the special role of the Spirit in our reception of the Word of God:

> Now we have received, not the spirit of the world, but the Spirit who is from God, so that we may know the things freely given to us by God, which things we also speak, not in words taught by human wisdom, but in those taught by the Spirit, combining spiritual thoughts with spiritual words. But a natural man does not accept the things of the Spirit of God, for they are foolishness to him; and he cannot understand them, because they are spiritually appraised. (1 Cor. 2:12–14)

When we devote ourselves to the apostles' teaching and to the Word of God, we are entering into an endeavor saturated with the Spirit of God.

The Spirit is intimately active in prayer. By His prompting, we address God intimately: "Abba, Father." We are further exhorted to "pray in the Spirit" (Jude 20). This is not a mindless prayer, but one cognizant of both His presence and our continuing dependence upon His grace and guidance. "For we do not know how to pray as we should, but the Spirit Himself intercedes for us with groanings too deep for words" (Rom. 8:26).

The Spirit is the architect of fellowship. Through His renewing work, He is drawing out a people from every tribe, nation, and tongue as an eternal community. As we devote ourselves to Christian fellowship, we are not merely entering into a human institution but engaging in sphere in which the Holy Spirit works powerfully through His people.

In exhorting the fellowship of believers in Corinth, Paul notes this enduring truth: "Do you not know that you are a temple of God and that the Spirit of God dwells in you?" (1 Cor. 3:16).[5]

These are the Holy Spirit's chosen, established means through which He conforms us to the image of Christ. By no means am I suggesting that the Holy Spirit can work only through these. The Holy Spirit is the Lord of all who "does whatever He pleases." He cannot be controlled by the precepts of man. Yet the question is not what the Lord can work through. For the purposes of sanctification, it is what He has revealed that He will and does work through. He has placed a perimeter of protection around His people, instructing us what we both should and shouldn't pursue in accordance with His purposes and for our good.

If we ignore the gracious means that God has given, we are guilty of neglecting our great salvation and grieving the Spirit of God. Conversely, availing ourselves of these endeavors will fill us with fresh supplies of grace and strength to progress.

Holocaust survivor Corrie Tenboom well observes: "When a Christian shuns fellowship with other Christians, the devil smiles. When he stops studying the Bible, the devil laughs. When he stops praying, the devil shouts for joy."[6]

## A FRAMEWORK, NOT A FORMULA

The spiritual endeavors that cause us to progress in our sanctification and spiritual growth are not quick fixes. In fact, their very nature mitigates against such. Rather than being a formula we can take like some sort of spiritual elixir, the Word of God, prayer, fellowship, and their manifold elements should be seen as a framework. The Spirit has established this framework, and when through faith and His leading we enter in, we experience the realm of His powerful changing grace. R. C. Sproul writes regarding the quest of spiritual maturity: "There are no quick and easy paths to spiritual maturity. The soul that seeks a deeper level of maturity must be prepared for a long arduous task. If we are to seek the kingdom of God, we must abandon any formulae that promise instant spiritual gratification."[7] While the task has its arduous elements, as the blood of the martyrs testifies, it also carries unspeakable joy. While we labor on this path, we are being taken further into the marvelous knowledge of Jesus Christ and all His benefits.

# HE WILL GLORIFY ME

There is a central goal to the work of the Holy Spirit that should cause us to check ourselves as to whether we are properly engaged in devoting ourselves to "the apostles teaching, to fellowship, to the breaking of bread, and to prayer." When our Lord outlined the coming of the Holy Spirit, He taught us there would be a clear indicator of the Comforter's redeeming and renewing work:

> But when He, the Spirit of truth, comes, He will guide you into all the truth; for He will not speak on His own initiative, but whatever He hears, He will speak; and He will disclose to you what is to come. He will glorify Me, for He will take of Mine and will disclose it to you. (John 16:13–14)

These spiritual endeavors are not ends unto themselves, but the means by which we behold the glory of Jesus Christ. Through the Scriptures, we are taken into the depths of the love, mercy, and grace He dispenses to His people. In prayer, we go before the throne of grace with our royal High Priest as our forerunner. In the devotion of Christian fellowship, we gather together around the glory of our risen Lord, worshipping Him, remembering His work and promise, and thanking Him for the provisions He has granted. This is the product of the Spirit because His purpose is to glorify the risen King. His purpose is to guide us to His glory and thereby purify us for His use. Therefore, we must take care to always remember that these endeavors are not an end unto themselves, but the means the Holy Spirit uses to reveal in us the unfolding glory of Jesus Christ.

## THE SIMPLE TRUTH

One may respond to the revelation of God's ordained means of sanctification with perplexity: "So that's it?" I acknowledge I am not proclaiming anything new, nor am I revealing something that has been kept secret. It is profoundly simple. *The Word of God, prayer*, and *fellowship*. These are the endeavors that God has established to which we devote ourselves. Through these, He conforms us to the image of Christ, sanctifying our very beings. It is only because of their simplicity and our lack of contentment that we often deem them as insufficient.

Lest we become lulled by the simplicity of these "means of grace," we must realize there is a radical power that resides in the faithful devotion to God's

Word, prayer, and fellowship. Far from being mundane, these devotions hold a myriad of profoundly purifying purposes. As we move on to further explore the intricacies and benefits of God's chosen way, we will behold with new eyes the importance of devoting ourselves to *His* sanctifying means.

---

[1] Through the rest of this work, "fellowship" and the "breaking of bread" will be dealt with as a whole. More exposition on these endeavors and their relationship and distinction will be addressed in chapter nine.

[2] Luke has been cultivating the fulfillment of the promise to pour out the Spirit on all people. The point that Luke chronicles in Acts 2 is the focal point of the book (whereas the cross and resurrection are the focal point of his gospel). To hold the position that Luke notes these things but is not presenting them in a prescriptive manner goes against both the immediate context and the overall narrative purpose of the book.

[3] By no means are these the only two other contexts in which one finds these means of grace. As one continues to explore the Word of God, these endeavors are continually presented as the prime devotions to which the community of Christ is to commit.

[4] J. C. Ryle, *Holiness* (Grand Rapids: Baker Book House 1979), 30.

[5] The Greek for "you" in this text is plural, further undergirding that the apostle is speaking about the community of believers and not the individual physical body.

[6] Corrie Tenboom, *Each New Day* (Grand Rapids: Revell, 2003), 178.

[7] R. C. Sproul, *The Soul's Quest for God* (Wheaton: Tyndale, 1992), 7.

# THE SIMPLE TRUTH

❧❦

And take . . . the sword of the Spirit, which is
the word of God.

Ephesians 6:17

7

# Unsheathing Our Swords

*Gripping the Spirit-Filled Power of the Word of God*

When you believed in Jesus of Nazareth, you enlisted. Using military language, Psalm 110 declares, "Your people will volunteer freely in the day of Your power" (v. 3). We have been called into service in the army of the King of Kings. Paul declares: "No soldier in active service entangles himself in the affairs of everyday life, so that he may please the one who enlisted him as a soldier" (2 Tim. 2:4). The path on which we proceed is marked with conflict—by our spiritual enemy, by this fallen world, and by the old self seeking to entangle us in sin. The only way we can proceed to conformity to the image of Christ is through the effectual equipping of God. He has provided all we need to engage in this war and emerge victorious.

The one who commissioned us also has equipped us with the necessary provisions to embark upon this divine quest for sanctification. The Spirit-filled center of all that has been granted is the Word of God. The Word is a veritable treasure of provision that we are called to utilize. Thus, let us proceed not only to

103

explore the enormous significance of the God-breathed Scriptures but also to establish every believer's dire need to devote himself to them.

The Word of God paints an array of imagery illustrating how the Scriptures powerfully work in the believer's life.

## THE SWORD OF THE SPIRIT

First, we will unsheathe the imagery of the Word as our sword. In Ephesians 6, Paul poetically exhorts us to be prepared for the onslaught of evil. "Therefore, take up the full armor of God, so that you will be able to resist in the evil day, and having done everything, to stand firm" (Eph. 6:13). We are to "put on" the breastplate of righteousness, the helmet of righteousness, and the shoes of the gospel of peace, and pick up the shield of faith. Putting on the full armor of God is analogous to living in Christ's victory and power. The final piece of wartime equipment is "the sword of the Spirit, which is the word of God" (6:17).

The first area of conflict against which the Word of God is effective is in the battle against our sinful desires. As we recognize the rebellious and ruinous impulses that arise within us, we are exhorted to confront them. Again the call is: "as aliens and strangers to abstain from fleshly lusts which wage war against the soul" (1 Peter 2:11). The manner in which we wage war is utilizing the Word of God. By growing in our knowledge of the Scriptures and becoming equipped with the knowledge of our salvation and the benefits of Christ's victory, we learn the proper way to wage war against fleshly lusts and sinful desires. We must plunge the sword of the Spirit into our enemy. By putting ourselves under the instruction and authority of God's Word, His sword will supernaturally penetrate the core of our being, both convicting us and conforming us to the image of Christ. "For the word of God is living and active and sharper than any two-edged sword, and piercing as far as the division of soul and spirit, of both joints and marrow, and able to judge the thoughts and intentions of the heart" (Heb. 4:12).

Remember, a sword is both an offensive and defensive weapon. Through wielding the Word of God, we are not only equipped to discern the presence of the seductive elements of evil but also overcome the onslaught of temptation. In the Scriptures, we are given two examples—one negative and one positive— of the need to properly utilize the sword of the Spirit when engaging the enemy.

## THE TECHNIQUE OF THE TEMPTER

In a lush garden, where every need and godly desire had its fulfillment, our first parents were met with temptation. They had received the Word of God: "The Lord God commanded the man, saying, 'From any tree of the garden you may eat freely; but from the tree of the knowledge of good and evil you shall not eat, for in the day that you eat from it you will surely die'" (Gen. 2:16). In the ideal environment, along came the Tempter: "And he said to the woman, "Indeed, has God said, 'You shall not eat from any tree of the garden'?" The woman responded by noting that the Lord proclaimed they could eat of any tree in the garden but the tree of the knowledge of good and evil.

Doing so would result in certain death. To this the Serpent responded: "You surely will not die! For God knows that in the day you eat from it your eyes will be opened, and you will be like God, knowing good and evil." Both of our first parents fell prey to temptation. They disobeyed the word of the Lord and plunged the world into sin and death.

We do well to note the technique of the Tempter here. First, the Serpent misquoted the Word of God. While God had declared they could eat of any tree save one, Satan said to Eve, "Has God said you shall not eat of any tree of the Garden?" The Enemy also denied the truthfulness of the Word of God. After Eve correctly informed the Serpent that eating of the forbidden tree would cause them to die because of their disobedience, he hissed the lie, "You surely shall not die!"

Our first parents fell because they refused to retain the Word of God and rather believed the lie of the Serpent. The techniques of the Tempter do not change. He appeals to our ungodly passions for the things of the world rather than the things of the Word. The apostle John notes how the elements that were used to entice Adam and Eve are still ongoing:

> For all that is in the world, the lust of the flesh and the lust of the eyes and the boastful pride of life, is not from the Father, but is from the world. And the world is passing away, and also its lusts; but the one who does the will of God abides forever. (1 John 2:16–17)

We are all sons and daughters of Adam and Eve. While the objects of weakness and manners of temptation vary, we carry on the family tradition of sin. Since the elements of enticement are still a painful reality, we must address the following question: How do we engage the enemy with the sword of the Spirit? While our first parents were weak and demonstrated how not to confront temptation, our Warrior arrived and not only overcame for us but taught us how to wield that weapon effectively.

## A LESSON IN SWORDSMANSHIP

In contrast to the lush garden with all the lavish surroundings, our Lord was led out to barren wilderness for a confrontation with the Serpent. He was not surrounded by a multitude of trees bearing nourishing fruit, but rather had not eaten for forty days and was surrounded by desolation. What He did have was sufficient to combat temptation, however, and He wielded it with marvelous precision.

The methods of the Serpent are familiar. To the weak and starving Jesus, the Serpent appealed to the lust of the eyes, the lust of the flesh, and the boastful pride of life. When confronted with the lust of the eyes by being promised inheriting the nations without taking up the cross and bowing to the devil instead, the Warrior countered: "You shall worship the Lord your God and serve Him only!" When the Tempter challenged Him the lust of the flesh, to turn stones into bread to satisfy His hunger, Jesus again deflected by stating the Scriptures: "Man does not live on bread alone but on every word that proceeds from the mouth of God!" Finally, in appealing to the boastful pride of life, the Serpent challenged the Savior to throw Himself off the temple to demonstrate that the angels would protect Him. Now Lord delivered His decisive final counterstrike: "You shall not tempt the

Lord Your God!" Unlike our first parents, our pure Prince, the Seed of the Woman,[1] deflected the Serpent's onslaught through properly wielding the Word of God and applying it with exacting precision.

Because the techniques of the Tempter do not change, the means of countering his ruinous onslaught effectively remain the same, as well. Learning from the example of our King, we must unsheathe the sword of the Spirit by devoting ourselves to the Word of God by placing ourselves under its teaching and actively bringing it into our lives.

## HANDLE WITH CARE

While the Word of God can be an unstoppable weapon in resisting temptation and proceeding on the path of purification, we must take care because misusing it will lead to ruin. Note what Peter declares of those who distort the Word of God:

> [O]ur beloved brother Paul, according to the wisdom given him, wrote to you, as also in all his letters, speaking in them of these things, in which are some things hard to understand, which the untaught and unstable distort, as they do also the rest of the Scriptures, to their own destruction. (2 Peter 3:15–16)

The sword of the Spirit is a weapon that will bring destruction upon those who misuse it. How do we ensure that we handle the Word with care and properly wield the sword for our good rather than our ruin?

First, it is absolutely necessary to receive this weapon in humility. We are called to put ourselves "under the Word," carefully considering what it teaches in order for the Spirit to use it as He wishes. We are not to try to force it to declare what we want. In James, we are exhorted:

> Therefore putting aside all filthiness and all that remains of wickedness, in humility receive the word implanted, which is able to save your souls. (Tim. 1:21)

In both the temptation accounts noted above, Satan misused the Word of God in His treacherous activities. While we must recognize this tool of the Tempter, we must also take heed that we don't willing participate in the distortion ourselves. While we all indeed "stumble in various ways," it is essential to for us to carefully consider the proper interpretation of the Scriptures. This is done through learning and applying the tried and true principles of biblical interpretation.[2] We do well to heed the warning to care for the sword so we will not be ashamed when we give account to our Commanding Officer:

> Be diligent to present yourself approved to God as a workman who does not need to be ashamed, handling accurately the word of truth. (2 Tim. 3:15)

## NEVER-ENDING RATIONS, EVER-BURNING LAMPS

In rebuking the onslaught of the Serpent, our Lord proclaimed another central purpose of the Scriptures. "Man does not live on bread alone, but on every word that proceeds from the mouth of God." The Scriptures are our spiritual nourishment. In his first epistle, Peter notes our need for the Word of God:

> [L]ike newborn babes, long for the pure milk of the word, that by it you may grow in respect to salvation. (1 Peter 2:2)

Just as pure milk is necessary for a newborn infant, so the purity of the Word of God is necessary for us. The result of frequently feeding upon the word is spiritual growth.

We are pilgrims progressing towards the kingdom. While we have the necessary rations to nourish us on our journey, we are also a displaced people walking in the midst of a world of darkness. Thankfully, our Lord has equipped us with an ever-burning lamp to light our way. In the beautiful Psalm that sings of the manifold blessings of God's Word, we read, "Thy word is a lamp unto my feet and a light unto my path" (Psalm 119:105).

When we refuse to pick up the lamp of the Word of God, we become prone to stumbling, as the path which we walk is not illuminated. When we refuse to feed upon our nourishing provision of the Scriptures, we will not grow and mature. The essence of the two concepts of the Scriptures, nourishment and light, are at work in the admonition of the author of Hebrews to grow to maturity in order to discern.

> For everyone who partakes only of milk is not accustomed to the word of righteousness, for he is a babe. But solid food is for the mature, who because of practice have their senses trained to discern good and evil. (Heb. 5:13–14)

110

The concern evident in this rebuke was that if one remained in a state of perpetual spiritual infancy, one would not be properly trained for discernment between good and evil. This would make this person a prime target for false teaching. The remedy is to "press on towards maturity" through becoming accustomed to the Word of Righteousness. A faithful devotion to the Word of God will cause growth. While the exact word-to-food analogy is distinct from the Peter passage we just explored,[3] the general growth imagery still applies. By progressing in our knowledge of God through His Word, we are taken further in the glories of the "great salvation" we have received and are given illumination regarding how to walk in God's chosen way.

The need to grow through the Word is related to our need to discern good from evil. The more we grow in the knowledge of Christ and His principles, the more we will have our paths illuminated so we may avoid the pitfalls that mark our course. The more we apply the Word's illuminating principles to our everyday lives, the further we will proceed in righteous living.

## THE ALL-IMPORTANT STEP

It is imperative that we keep in focus the targeted goal of our Scriptural endeavors. The Word of God is not a mantra simply to be memorized but a means of recognizing righteousness and resisting sin by fixing our eyes on the one who sustains and leads us in victory. We need to both carefully read the Scriptures and proceed with the all-important task of bringing it into action. The wisdom of James resonates on this point:

111

> But prove yourselves doers of the word, and not merely hearers who delude themselves. For if anyone is a hearer of the word and not a doer, he is like a man who looks at his natural face in a mirror; for once he has looked at himself and gone away, he has immediately forgotten what kind of person he was. But one who looks intently at the perfect law, the law of liberty, and abides by it, not having become a forgetful hearer but an effectual doer, this man will be blessed in what he does. (James 1:22–25)

This call is for all the commissioned ones: Be an effectual doer and be blessed. In doing so, the Word of God will saturate every aspect of our lives and, by the power of the Spirit who dwells within us, lead us in the way everlasting. May we emulate King David's example in our quest for conformity to the image of Christ: "Your word I have treasured in my heart, that I may not sin against You" (Psalm 119:11).

## GRASP YOUR SWORD

A warning siren resounds for all who are on the path the pilgrims trod. Too many have their swords sheathed. Spiritual famine through willing neglect of the Word is a pandemic throughout the Christian community. Many have covered the lamp that lights the way, putting them in danger of stumbling.

In the Word of God, we have the Spirit-filled provisions necessary to fight the temptations that confront us, to feed upon His rich knowledge, and to illuminate the path of which we walk. We are surrounded by dangers without and enemies within. Our Lord Himself, in His prayer to His Father, established the means used to set apart His people. "Sanctify them by the truth. Thy word is truth" (John 17:17).

Therefore, let us forsake our self-sufficient attitudes and endless excuses and turn to God's gracious gift and continually avail ourselves of the powerful, sanctifying provisions granted through the Word of Christ.

---

[1] The "duel in the desert" has profound theological significance. First, there was the promise that the "Seed of the woman" would come and crush the Serpent's head. While this essentially occurred at the cross, the temptation was significant in that through suffering, Jesus was perfected as the second Adam, who was the head of the new human race that would be atoned by His sacrifice (Heb. 2:10). See Paul's establishing of these points in Romans 5 and 1 Corinthians 15.

[2] The milk imagery functions differently in both 1 Peter and Hebrews. In 1 Peter, the word is presented as being as necessary for spiritual growth as a mother's milk is for an infant. In Hebrews, milk is contrasted with "solid food" in order to exhort readers to advance to maturity.

With all prayer and petition pray at all times in the Spirit, and with this in view, be on the alert with all perseverance and petition for all the saints.

Ephesians 6:18

# 8

# Approaching the Throne of Grace

*The Purifying Power of Prayer*

"**P**ray without ceasing."

"Pray for one another."

"Pray at all times in the Spirit."

"Pray." (1 Thessalonians 5:17; James 5:16; Ephesians 6:18; Matthew 6:9

Do you hear the call? As Christians, these Scriptures are not options for us. Rather they line up outside the dwelling place of God and, like the blast of a trumpet, command us to go before our Royal Father. In light of our Savior's entrance into the presence of the Most High through the blood of the Eternal Covenant, we have received a divine summons.

> Therefore let us draw near with confidence to the throne of grace, so that we may receive mercy and find grace to help in time of need. (Heb. 4:16)

Prayer is an endeavor that stirs up several stilted concepts: Hands folded. Heads bowed. Eyes closed. While reverence is indeed a necessary attitude of

115

prayer, the divine devotion has nothing to do with the position of your body. It is about our thoughts, our feelings, and our entreaties entering the very throne room of God. Through prayer, we enter the hidden realm and have been given the privilege of approaching the "throne of grace." Through this "drawing near," we become further recipients of God's unfolding mercy and grace.

## PRAYER WITH THE TRIUNE GOD

Prayer is communication with God. God, as revealed through the teaching of the Son, is one in essence but three in person: the Father, the Son, and the Holy Spirit. Our triune God is intimately involved in the prayers of His people. As we lift our petitions and praises, we have been given a behind-the-scenes look into what occurs in the spiritual realm during our communication with our Creator. We have a wondrous, inspiring view of how God, in His fullness, is involved in the endeavor of prayer.

The Son has sent the Spirit into the world in order to draw us to the Father. The Holy Spirit draws us to Jesus, who is our eternal High Priest. It is through Him that we draw near to the throne of the Almighty. In Hebrews, we read of our radical new standing before God and how our relationship with Him has been forever revolutionized through Jesus' intercessory work:

> Therefore, brethren, since we have confidence
> to enter the holy place by the blood of Jesus, by a
> new and living way which He inaugurated for
> us through the veil, that is, His flesh, and since
> we have a great priest over the house of God, let

116

> us draw near with a sincere heart in full
> assurance of faith, having our hearts sprinkled
> clean from an evil conscience and our bodies
> washed with pure water. (Heb. 10:19–22)

Because we have the perfect priest with the perfect sacrifice who is forever raised and who will eternally intercede for us, we are able to draw near in "full assurance." We know our sins are forgiven and we are forever secure in His continuing grace.

It is foundational that we have these truths anchored in our hearts when we enter His presence. It is only because we have this great High Priest that we dare enter into His courts. As we enter the heavenly throne room, we do well to realize that God—the Father, the Son, and the Holy Spirit—is actively involved in all of the various facets of prayer. *The Spirit* fuels us and guides us in our prayers, often in ways with which we are not consciously aware (Rom. 8:26–27). *The Son* has taken His eternal place as our intercessor, and through Him we are taken into the heavenly courts. And we go before *the Father*, who is our merciful caretaker and grace-giver. While our eyes do not behold these glories, when we enter into the blessed endeavor of prayer, we are engaged in an activity in which the fullness of God is intimately working with His created subjects. When we faithfully enter His presence, we are being molded by hands of the Sovereign Lord.

With this as the behind-the-scenes reality of prayer, we must ask how we are to pray. What is the proper attitude? What does the Lord want us to pray for? What are the principles that have been laid down in the Scriptures that define effectiveness in prayer?

Remember, we are entering the throne room of the King of the universe, who holds all things together by His mere word. In light of this humbling honor, we are called to be both actively engaged and properly applying our King's guidance to progress in our pursuit of holiness.

## TEACH US TO PRAY

Jesus is the great High Priest after the order of Melchizedek.[1] He fulfills the office of the perfect priest and serves as our forerunner into the presence of God. Jesus is also the "prophet," fulfilling God's promise to send one like and even greater than Moses to guide the people of God in proper worship of the Most High. This promise is recorded in Deuteronomy 18:15: "The Lord your God will raise up for you a prophet like me [Moses] from among you, from your countrymen, you shall listen to him." The Prophet arrived, taught, and through His wisdom we are granted the proper way to approach our Sovereign Lord.

There have been numerous teachers who purport to reveal the "secret" of prayer. These techniques consist of various props and elements to establish narrow prescriptions drawn out for continuous repetition. All these promise us the enabling power to draw "nearer" to God. The fact is, we are able to enter the throne room whenever we want through the intercession of Jesus Christ. Rather than consulting so-called wisdom or engaging in treacherous techniques, let us sit at our Master's feet and heed His teaching.

The initial disciples gathered around their Lord and presented Him with a simple request: "Teach us to pray" (Luke 11:1). While the following passage has been given the label the Lord's Prayer, it is more rightly defined as the Disciple's Prayer, as this is intended to be for the fallen yet faithful children of God.[2] Jesus granted their request, and in turn, gives all of God's children the guiding wisdom of a prayer pleasing to the Father. When we pray in the way Christ has commanded, we are following His righteous guidance, and our prayers will be filled with the Spirit. Our Teacher begins:

> "Pray, then, in this way: 'Our Father who art in heaven, Hallowed be Thy name. Thy kingdom come. Thy will be done, on earth as it is in heaven." (Matt. 6:9–10)

First and foremost, we are given the privilege of calling God *our Father*. In fact, this is how Jesus teaches us to pray. Our relationship is radically changed through the work of the Son so that all who approach God through Jesus now do so as His children. And His children's primary concern is regarding the "name" of the Father. The name of God is not simply the word or words by which we call Him. It is representative of His character and purposes.[2] When we pray in the name of the Lord, we are aligning ourselves with His purposes and His will, thus we pray *"Thy* will be done." In doing this, and as the Holy Spirit continually changes us to want what God wants, we become conformed to His image. Our chief concern is to be for His glory and for His name to hallowed by all. Because this is our chief concern, we pray for the day when this will fully occur: "Thy Kingdom to come." In the opening to His exemplary prayer, the Master is teaching us about what our priorities should be: our relationship with God Almighty and our desire for His glorification and honor. With these established, the prayer now turns to our petitions as we wait for His coming:

> "Give us this day our daily bread. And forgive us our debts, as we also have forgiven our debtors." (Matt. 6:11–12)

In light of the emphasis on the holiness of the Lord and our longing for His kingdom, the prayer now moves to the recognition of our weakness and utter dependence on God. We are dependant upon His providing power in all areas of life. If we are dependant upon Him for bread, how much more are we dependent upon Him for the greater things? As we confess, "forgive us our debts," we acknowledge total dependence on His redeeming power for forgiveness. Since we are still sinners, sustained by God's grace, striving towards the kingdom of God, we call upon Him in our walk:

> "And do not lead us into temptation, but deliver us from evil." (Matt. 6:13)

In this world, we have a dire need for His guidance and deliverance. This only comes from the throne of grace. We are blind apart from His guiding light, and we petition for His *leading away* from temptation and *deliverance out* of evil.

Our Master, in simple, straightforward fashion, grants us a profound template for our prayers as we approach the throne of grace. This is not necessarily a prayer to be recited verbatim, though this is certainly permissible if its meaning is expressed. It is more an exemplary prayer that highlights the manner and essence of the kind of faithful prayer that will "avail much." By following our Savior and Teacher's guidance, we should fix our eyes foremost on the glory of our God and the fame of His name, while acknowledging our perpetual shortcomings and utter dependence on Him. If these take root in our lives and are expressed in our perpetual prayers, He will continually conform us to His glorious image.

## TEACH US HOW *NOT* TO PRAY

Our wise Master has instructed us regarding the proper way to pray. He also has revealed perilous manners of prayer. There are improper ways to approach the Lord of Hosts. He commands us:

> "When you pray, you are not to be as the hypocrites; for they love to stand and pray in the synagogues and on the street corners, in order to be seen by men. Truly I say to you, they have their reward in full. But you, when you pray, go into your inner room, and when you have shut your door, pray to your Father who is in secret, and your Father who sees in secret will repay you." (Matt. 6:4–5)

The way of the Master is to humbly approach the King. The way of man is to pray to obtain praise or stature in human eyes and from human lips. To use the gift of approaching God as a means of external gain is an outworking of faithlessness. This does not mean public prayer is forbidden but that our attitudes must be grounded in humility. Jesus continues:

> "When you are praying, do not use meaningless repetition, as the Gentiles do, for they suppose that they will be heard for their many words.

> Therefore do not be like them; for your Father
> knows what you need, before you ask Him."
> (Matt. 6:6–9)

If we think that we can find a proper formula, repeat it, and cause God to answer us, this is demonstrative of an impenitent attitude. This is an act that, either consciously or unconsciously, places our power in the center and God as the servant. Rather, an attitude of dependence is necessary because the Lord knows what we need well before we ask Him.

The underlying attitude that Jesus is teaching us to avoid is pride. We are presented with two attitudes that can accompany us as we go before the Judge of all: We can enter with humility, recognizing our utter dependence on God and His Christ or we can approach with the perilous attitude of pride. We are promised: "God is opposed to the proud, but gives grace to the humble" (James 4:6). Let us forsake the perils of pride and follow the way instructed by the Master.

## THE SPECTRUMS OF PRAYER

Have you ever watched a jeweler inspect a precious gemstone? While from a distance the jewel holds a certain beauty, through close inspection, the finer characteristics and color prisms become even more apparent. Our relationship with God, which is more precious than any earthly thing, finds its full expression in the endeavor of prayer. Like a jewel, this activity is filled with spectra that radiate a fully engaged, God-centered way of life.

The Scriptures place a prime emphasis on thanksgiving. Over and over, we are exhorted to lift our voices in thankfulness to the Lord. Thanksgiving is the product of a heart of faithfulness. It is the outworking of a heart that realizes the overwhelming intensity of God's grace. "Surely the righteous will give thanks to Your name; the upright will dwell in Your presence" (Psalm 140:13). When we reflect on just how deep the grace of God runs, and even though our finite minds only take in a small sip of its unending river, our hearts cannot help but overflow with thanksgiving. In exhorting us to be filled with the Spirit, Paul notes our continuing practice is to be "always giving thanks for all things in the name of our Lord Jesus Christ to God, even the Father" (Eph. 5:20).

Intimately related to thanksgiving is praise. As we approach the throne of grace with Jesus as a forerunner: "Through Him then, let us continually offer up a sacrifice of praise to God, that is, the fruit of lips that give thanks to His name" (Heb. 13:5). Praising His name is an intimate aspect of prayer. When we go before His throne and praise His name, we express our adoration for our King. The Psalms are peppered with calls to praise. "Praise the Lord! Praise the name of the Lord; Praise Him, O servants of the Lord" (Psalm 135:1).

A purifying aspect of prayer is confession. Jesus laid this foundation in His teaching on prayer, and this is echoed by one of the disciples that initially sat at His feet: "If we confess our sins, He is faithful and righteous to forgive us our sins and purify us from all unrighteousness" (1 John 1:9). Confessing our sins before the Lord is a necessary step in our cleansing. As we go before the throne of mercy and grace, we carry our confessed sins to our great High Priest, who ever intercedes for us. By confessing our wretchedness and His righteousness, we are purified by His priestly presence.

Finally, petition is a commanded facet of our prayer life. God wants us to humbly carry our petitions before Him. "Be anxious for nothing, but in everything by prayer and supplication with thanksgiving let your requests be made known to God" (Phil. 4:6). Our Father is our caretaker. He delights in giving His children good and perfect gifts. But we must again take care to examine our motives, whether we are pursuing selfish ambition or godly gain. James explains both our need to ask and our need to do so in humility: "You do not have because you do not ask. You ask and do not receive, because you ask with wrong motives, so that you may spend it on your pleasures" (James 4:2–3).

It is the Father's good pleasure to give His children that which is good. Since He is the one who knows our ultimate good, we must learn from our Lord Jesus who, though being in very nature sinless and pure, still amended His prayer with "Nevertheless, not My will but Thy will [be done]" (Matt. 26:39).

As we peer into the many spectra of prayer, it becomes apparent that although prayer is simply communication with God, it is also a complex endeavor. If our life of prayer is to be whole, we do well to incorporate all of these elements. By approaching the throne of grace, we enter a matrix where our relationship with God is magnified. It is where true worship results, and thus *we are changed.*

## THE CONFORMING PURPOSE OF PRAYER

Be sure, prayer is not a means to change God. The throne of grace is a place where we are changed *by* God. This is not a sphere from which one will emerge unaffected. Through learning what He desires from us, and through properly praying in His name, we go into the purifying presence of the Most High. In prayer, our desires are made known. Like David, we recognize that He knows our hearts more than we. We are to concur with the ancient king in petitioning, "Search me, O God, and know my heart; try me and know my anxious thoughts; and see if there be any hurtful way in me, and lead me in the everlasting way (Psalm 139:23–24).

In prayer, God's glory is demonstrated. Through our praises and worship, we experience in a very real way the glory for which we were redeemed. In prayer, His holiness is manifested. None truly enter His presence without realizing, "Holy, Holy, Holy is the Lord God Almighty who was and is and is to come" (Rev. 4:8). In prayer, the great gulf that separates the common from the holy is both highlighted and bridged. Prayer humbles. Prayer motivates. Prayer purifies.

## THE CONTINUAL CALL TO PRAYER

The royal trumpet call goes forth. "Rejoice always; pray without ceasing; in everything give thanks; for this is God's will for you in Christ Jesus" (1 Thess. 5:16–18). We have a standing invitation to go before the throne of grace. It is God's will that we come before His majestic presence with a heart of thanksgiving for all He has done, is doing, and will do in our lives. Though we were once outcast enemies, He has transferred us into His eternal family, and through the Spirit we now address Him as our intimate Father. With Christ as our forerunner, and with attitudes of thanksgiving and dependence rooted firmly in our hearts, may we continue our quest for conformity to the image of Christ through the manifold endeavor of prayer.

---

[1] The reason that I think it is more rightly defined as the Disciples' Prayer is that it is what we, as His followers, are to pray. This is not a prayer that Jesus would have prayed, as it petitions for the forgiveness of sins. Being perfect and sinless, this does not reflect His reality. Though it called the Lord's Prayer because He taught it, if we were to label a Scriptural account as the Lord's Prayer, I think John 17 is a much better candidate.

[2] See chapter eight of my work *Eternal Scars* (Bellefonte, PA: Strong Tower Publishing, 2011) for a more in-depth discussion on the nature of praying in the name of Jesus.

# Approaching the Throne of Grace

✌✎

Do you not know that you are a temple of God
and that the Spirit of God dwells in you?

1 Corinthians 3:16

9

# Drawing Near the Flame of Fellowship

*The Purifying Power of Devotion to the Community of Christ*

There is a story circulating in pastoral circles that has become somewhat of a legend. This tale appears to have its origins in Europe during the nineteenth century. Word had reached a certain preacher that one of his parishioners had decided that church attendance, the partaking of communal prayer, and proclamation of the Word of God were not necessary. On a cold, dreary day, the preacher set out with his staff to attempt to draw back the one who had gone astray.

The quest to bring this man back to the fold did not even require the preacher to utter a single word. As the preacher walked into the parishioner's house, the man was quite sure of his visitor's intent. The preacher was going to try to talk him back to church. The preacher did no such thing. Instead, he noticed an oven full of red-hot coals intent on warming the bitterly cold surroundings. Walking over to the oven, he grabbed a pair of tongs and extracted a solitary piece of coal from the fire. The coal burned a brilliant matrix of reds and yellows as the preacher walked over and placed it on the table in front of the man. They both watched as the brilliance faded and the heat rescinded from the piece. Soon it was cold, dark, and useless. The preacher's eyes locked onto his wayward parishioner's and nothing more needed to be said.

"I will be back on Sunday," responded the convicted man. "Thanks for the fiery sermon."

Whatever be the reasons, devotion to fellowship has become *passé* in the minds of many believers. Rather than being seen as an essential cog of the faith, it is more frequently viewed as a beneficial, albeit unnecessary, facet of the Christian life. The truth is, when we are isolated from Christian fellowship, we distance ourselves from an essential outlet of the purifying power of the Holy Spirit.

## WHAT IS TRUE FELLOWSHIP?

Before exploring the spiritual power at the root of fellowship, we must come to a clear definition of true *biblical* fellowship. There are many who gather under the banner of Jesus Christ. A vast array of communities claim Christ. On one end, there are those who gather under a false gospel and a false assurance of eternal life. In essence, these are those who gather in the name of the Messiah yet are void of the Spirit of God. Fellowship under this banner is fruitless.[1] On the other end are the "called out ones," those who adhere to the true gospel of Jesus Christ and walk according to His statutes. Our fellowship is defined first and foremost by our relationship with Christ.

John establishes this truth in the opening to his first epistle:

> What we have seen and heard we proclaim to you also, so that you too may have fellowship with us; and indeed our fellowship is with the Father, and with His Son Jesus Christ. (1 John 1:3)

The two seals that must be present in any authentic gathering of God's people are a devotion to the Word and a devotion to prayer. In essence, true biblical fellowship is gathering around the common salvation we have in Christ Jesus. A devotion to the faith delivered "once for all" is its heartbeat. We have a common source of guidance, teaching, and revelation in the Scriptures. We have a common goal in pursuing the glories of our renewed relationship with our Maker through prayer. If these two are absent, the genuineness of fellowship is brought into question. Conversely, with these established, we have a starting point for the glorious pursuit of purification through the Spirit-filled endeavor of fellowship.

A. W. Tozer paints an appropriate picture of the essence of true fellowship.

> Has it ever occurred to you that one hundred pianos all tuned to the same fork are automatically tuned to each other? They are of one accord by being tuned, not to each other, but to another standard to which each one must individually bow. So one hundred worshipers [meeting] together, each one looking away to Christ, are in heart nearer to each other than

they could possibly be, were they to become 'unity' conscious and turn their eyes away from God to strive for closer fellowship.[2]

It is the common faith in our King and His redemptive work that is the proper starting point for biblical fellowship. While this is our tuning fork, the Spirit has also equipped His people with distinct gifts that produce His sovereign symphony that fills the temple of the living God.

## THE TABERNACLE AND THE TEMPLE

In the midst of forming the nation of Israel, God instituted a tent, or tabernacle, through which His special presence would dwell in the midst of His people. There was a vast array of rites and commands instituted in the building, care, and use of this house. We are informed through the teaching of the Scriptures that the Holy Spirit would come upon certain people to equip them with the skills to build and administer service in the dwelling place of God.

> Then Moses said to the sons of Israel, "See, the Lord has called by name Bezalel the son of Uri, the son of Hur, of the tribe of Judah. And He has filled him with the Spirit of God, in wisdom, in understanding and in knowledge and in all craftsmanship . . . Now Bezalel and Oholiab, and every skillful person in whom the Lord has put skill and understanding to know how to perform all the work in the construction of the sanctuary, shall perform in accordance with all that the Lord has commanded." (Ex. 35:30–31, 36:1)

This service continued when the temple came into existence. However, once Jesus accomplished His redemptive work and sent His Spirit, a radically new temple was created for the living God. Speaking to the church of Corinth, Paul states: "Do you not know that you are a temple of God and that the Spirit of God dwells in you? If any man destroys the temple of God, God will destroy him, for the temple of God is holy, and that is what you are" (1 Cor. 3:16, 17). The "you" here is plural. There were those who were causing illegitimate division and strife in the community and disrupting the edifying work of fellowship. The gathering of believers is a sphere of grace to all gathering under its banner. This temple of the Spirit is where lives are transformed.

Through the fellowship of believers, God's Spirit dwells. Unlike the times before the coming of Christ, when the Spirit would come to equip only certain individuals of the faithful to build and minister, now all have been given the Spirit of the living God to edify each other in conformity to the image of Christ.

## SPIRITUAL GIFTS

Why gather together? Why go through the process of fellowship when so much of the time heartache accompanies community? First, it is a command. "Do not forsake the gathering together" (Heb. 10:24). One of the prime reasons the Lord exhorts us not to forsake fellowship (or our gathering together) is that His Spirit works through the gifts He grants His children. The Holy Spirit sovereignly grants spiritual gifts for the edification of the body of Christ, both individually and corporately.

The most prominent passage that addresses the nature and work of spiritual gifts in found in 1 Corinthians 12.

> Now there are varieties of gifts, but the same Spirit. And there are varieties of ministries, and the same Lord. There are varieties of effects, but the same God who works all things in all persons. But to each one is given the manifestation of the Spirit for the common good. (1 Cor. 12:4–7)

Each and every individual is given a manifestation of the Spirit. This manifestation, given the context, is the specific, gifted outworking given for the edification of the Church as a whole. All are gifted in various ways, with various ministries, but there is a central, essential definition of a spiritual gift. It is given to the one for the edification of the other. It doesn't matter what gift was given or to whom it was given. The Spirit's common intent is that each gift is given for the mutual benefit of the Church. If you are Christ's, then you have been granted a gift intended for use. Likewise, there is a vast called-out community that has been gifted to serve you. The collective endeavor towards conformity to the image of Jesus Christ and the beholding of His glory, when combined with the diversity of gifts given, forms a spiritual symphony.

> Now you are Christ's body, and individually members of it. And God has appointed in the church, first apostles, second prophets, third teachers, then miracles, then gifts of healings, helps, administrations, various kinds of tongues. All are not apostles, are they? All are

not prophets, are they? All are not teachers, are
they? All are not workers of miracles, are they?
All do not have gifts of healings, do they? All
do not speak with tongues, do they? All do not
interpret, do they? But earnestly desire the
greater gifts. And I show you a still more
excellent way. (1 Cor. 12:27–31)

We are commanded to accept the diversity of gifts, as it
is the sovereign right of the Spirit to build His people
the way He sees fit. In light of His purpose and gifting,
Paul exhorts us to walk a "more excellent way." What is
this way of which Paul speaks?

## A More Excellent Way

We often get distracted in the running of our spiritual
race to the kingdom. We may find ourselves distracted
by enviously looking toward others and their gifts and
take our eyes off the prize. Recall when the disciples
were conversing after the resurrection and Peter was
so concerned with what would become of the apostle
John. Peter inquired of the risen Christ: "Lord, what
about this man?" Jesus said to him, "If I want him to
remain until I come, what is that to you? You follow
Me!" *You follow me.* A command given to Peter, yet
implied to every one of us. We must fix our eyes on
Christ, not envying others but rather emulating His
example. Then we will walk a more excellent way. We
will live our lives and exercise our spiritual gifts with
the all-important attitude of love.

Paul continues his exhortation on spiritual
gifts by both defining and describing what love is and
how love acts. Only with this divine trait fueling our
fellowship will the goal be accomplished.

> If I speak with the tongues of men and of angels, but do not have love, I have become a noisy gong or a clanging cymbal. If I have the gift of prophecy, and know all mysteries and all knowledge; and if I have all faith, so as to remove mountains, but do not have love, I am nothing. And if I give all my possessions to feed the poor, and if I surrender my body to be burned, but do not have love, it profits me nothing. Love is patient, love is kind and is not jealous; love does not brag and is not arrogant, does not act unbecomingly; it does not seek its own, is not provoked, does not take into account a wrong suffered, does not rejoice in unrighteousness, but rejoices with the truth; bears all things, believes all things, hopes all things, endures all things. Love never fails. (1 Cor. 13:1–8)

This is a familiar passage, but while most of us are accustomed to hearing it in the context of marriage or romantic love, notice that it is actually written as part of Paul's exhortation to fellowship and use of the spiritual gifts. While these gifts come from the Spirit of God, they become effectual only when fueled by the divine trait of love. When this occurs, the purifying power of the Spirit will accomplish sanctifying works beyond our comprehension. *Love never fails.*

D. A. Carson comments on Paul's poetic declaration:

> If Paul were addressing the modern church, perhaps he would extrapolate further: You Christians who prove spirituality by the amount of theological information you can cram into your heads, I tell you that such knowledge by itself proves nothing. And you

who affirm the Spirit's presence in your meetings because there is a certain style of worship (whether formal and stately or exuberant and spontaneous) if your worship patterns are not expressions of love, you are spiritually bankrupt.[3]

Love must characterize our fellowship. The apostle John minces no words in stating such: "Beloved, let us love one another, for love is from God; and everyone who loves is born of God and knows God. The one who does not love does not know God, for God is love" (1 John 4:7–8). We must take care not to confuse the world's definition of love with the divine definition: "In this is love, not that we loved God, but that He loved us and sent His Son to be the propitiation for our sins" (1 John 4:10).

It is this love, brothers and sisters, around which we gather. This is the context in which we grow. Love that produces pure fellowship is not based on emotional whims, but on what God has done for us. As we grow in this realization and utilize our spiritual gifts with this as its purifying center, we are walking the way which will lead to the edification of the Church.

## GIFTED TO GROW

"Edification" is a biblical term used to describe the end result of the use of the spiritual gifts. The imagery is of the building up of a structure. When the Scriptures declare, "Let all things be done for edification" (1 Cor. 14:26), it is a challenge and command for the redeemed to be active, with love as their spiritual fuel, in building up the temple of God, His people. You have been granted a gift that is meant for use. You have been given a role in this grand construction project that spans the ages. All of us have been provided with various tools for this project from the provider and architect of it all.

Fellowship is a matrix of spiritual life in which we give and receive for the purpose of growing in the love and grace of the one who loved us and gave Himself for us. Since He is surely returning and we will give account for what we have been given, may we be active and diligent so we hear those blessed words He has promised those who were faithful with what they were given: "Well done, good and faithful servant, enter the into the joy of your Master" (Matt. 25:23).

## THE COMMAND OF COMMUNION

As we await the day we meet our Master face to face, He has given us a meal for our spiritual benefit. Recall that those who were walking by the Spirit were devoting themselves to "the breaking of bread" (Acts 2:42). A great deal of controversy has accompanied this observance we know as communion. While this confusion and conflict have often cast a shadow over this observance, the fact is we are commanded as a community to participate.

There are two distinct aspects to the Lord's Supper that, once recognized and observed, become a powerful means through which the Spirit works. This does not mean there is some mystical power in the elements themselves. The power is in that to which these elements point in regards to the King. These two aspects are *remembrance* and *looking for His return*.

During the final Passover meal Jesus ate with His disciples, just prior to the ultimate Passover, the

Lamb of God instituted this meal of remembrance. "When He had taken some bread and given thanks, He broke it, and gave it to them, saying, 'This is My body which is given for you; do this in remembrance of Me.' And in the same way He took the cup after they had eaten, saying, 'This cup which is poured out for you is the new covenant in My blood'" (Luke 22:19–20). God has instituted various signs that point to His promises in order that we might bring these to remembrance.[4] Our King has given us this command in order that we remember. As we progress, we cannot lose sight of the cross, where the ultimate Passover occurred. By partaking in the act of communion, we together are continually proclaiming the act that has eternally atoned.

As we progress in conformity to the image of Christ, we are continually looking back at our common source of sanctification—the historical fact that the death and resurrection of Jesus was *for us*. We are demonstrating that we are His people who have been delivered by His blood and are looking toward the day we fully enter His joy. Paul highlights this second aspect of the Lord's table:

> For as often as you eat this bread and drink the cup, you proclaim the Lord's death until He comes. (1 Cor. 11:26)

The meal over which Jesus presided consisted of the first three cups and concluded with the third. Our Lord paused at the fourth and final cup, declaring, "But I say to you, I will not drink of this fruit of the vine from now on until that day when I drink it new with you in My Father's kingdom" (Matt. 26:29). The fourth cup will be drunk when Jesus returns. As we take the cup, we remember His death and look forward to His return.[5]

The meal of remembrance is a time for us to gather. Its elements represent the once-for-all sacrifice that eternally cleanses us, the work of Jesus Christ, which is the unending tie binding us together. It also causes us to pause and look forward to the day when we all enter the kingdom and Jesus drinks the fourth cup of final fulfillment when we forever will feast together in the Father's kingdom.

## THE CARAVAN TO THE KINGDOM

God has not placed us on the path alone. While it is true we all must carry our own loads (Gal. 6:5), we all are part of a grand caravan to the kingdom. When the ancients traveled across the wilderness, they would do so by caravan. There are several reasons for this. The presence of many would serve to assist when one fell ill or injured, thus allowing them to "[bear] one another's burdens" (Gal. 6:1). If one would run dry of food or water, those with abundance would share. The wilderness was also filled with ravenous beasts lurking to take prey that crossed into their domain. In traveling by community, the dangers were thwarted. Likewise, those who place themselves into Christian fellowship find shelter from the sinister forces that seek their ruin. In fact, when one was placed outside the sphere of fellowship, Paul declared they were "delivered unto Satan" (1 Cor. 5:5). It is therefore essential that we embark upon our journey through the gift of Christian fellowship, as we will not only progress in conformity to Christ's image but also be granted protection from the perils of journeying alone.

As we walk by the Spirit to the kingdom of God, we learn very quickly that this is not an easy journey. Rather, in following Jesus, He declares to any one desiring to be His disciple, "If anyone wishes to come after Me, he must deny himself, and take up his cross daily and follow Me" (Luke 9:23). Suffering is not pleasant, but it is a reality that holds a purifying purpose in the life of all God's commissioned children. We now proceed to explore the scriptural reasons for the "stones in our shoes."

---

[1] There certainly isn't room to provide even a partial list of such. The truth is that ever since the birth of the Church, there have been those who claim the name of Christ yet deny the essence of the gospel. Paul, in 1 Corinthians 15:1–8, outlines the essential beliefs that unite the Church. He declares if the death of Christ for our sins and the resurrection from the dead is denied, "You have believed in vain." There are certainly other issues that have inseparable attachments to the gospel (the deity of Christ, salvation by faith alone, and so on). In light of this, we must continually walk the way of discernment, "testing the spirits."

[2] A. W. Tozer, *The Pursuit of God* (New York: Christian Publications, 1982), 97.

[3] D. A. Carson, *Showing the Spirit* (Grand Rapids: Baker, 1984), 61.

[4] There are numerous other signs that God has instituted for remembrance: the rainbow, circumcision, the Passover meal, and the stone raised by Joshua, just to name a few. The ultimate signs of eternal remembrance are the scars that remain of the body of Christ from the cross.

[5] There is some dispute regarding the fourth cup. Some postulate that is was actually drunk at the supper. However, given the evidence, in my estimation it is most compelling that the fourth cup was never drunk as a sign of an event that is yet to be fulfilled—the marriage supper of the Lamb.

❧❧

All discipline for the moment seems not to be joyful, but sorrowful; yet to those who have been trained by it, afterwards it yields the peaceful fruit of righteousness.

Hebrews 12:11

# 10

# The Stones in Our Shoes

*The Purpose of Suffering on the Pilgrim's Path*

Why? The question has echoed through the annals of human history. Why is there evil in the lives of God's chosen ones? Why do we suffer? Why does hardship so often cross our path? There is no prohibition against asking such questions. In fact, there are numerous examples in the Scriptures of the faithful doing just that. However, in seeking answers, it is imperative that we maintain the proper attitude.

There has been an alarming reversal, especially in the last few centuries, in the manner in which we approach the Almighty. C. S. Lewis well noted this irreverent attitude in his work *God in the Dock*.

> The ancient man approached God (or even the gods) as the accused person approaches his judge. For the modern man the roles are reversed. He is the judge: God is in the dock. He is a quite kindly judge: if God should have a reasonable defence for being the god who permits war, poverty and disease, he is ready to listen to it. The trial may even end in God's acquittal. But the important things is Man is on the Bench and God is in the Dock.[1]

Lewis' sarcastic tone hits its mark. *We* are the corrupted ones going before the righteous, sovereign Lord of creation. *We* are the ones in the defendant's box. The mere fact that we dare go into the presence of the Mighty One at all should cause fear and trembling. With ourselves placed firmly in the defendant's seat, we, in humility and by His grace, may ask why there are "stones in our shoes" on the path that produces sanctification.

## CONSIDER IT ALL JOY

There is a command given to the commissioned community regarding how we are to respond to trials and suffering. On the surface, this command is peculiar. We are exhorted to "[c]onsider it all joy, my brethren, when you encounter various trials " (James 1:2). The world's response to suffering is to despair; the believer's response is to rest in joy. Why would we be commanded to be joyful in the midst of sorrow?

A more terrifying prospect than suffering itself is meaningless suffering. Where there is no meaning, there is no purpose. But there is radical purpose for the trials that accompany the believer's walk. In continuing his command to consider trials to be a joyful endeavor, James notes that the testing of our faith produces endurance. "And let endurance have its perfect result, so that you may be perfect and complete, lacking in nothing" (1:3–4).

Where there is no purpose, there is no hope. Thankfully, our God has lavished His sovereign wisdom upon our lives and we can rest and rejoice in the fact that nothing is outside the realm of God's conforming purpose. In Romans, we read of a similar chain to that in James:

> Not only this, but we also exult in our tribulations, knowing that tribulation brings about perseverance; and perseverance, proven character; and proven character, hope; and hope does not disappoint, because the love of God has been poured out within our hearts through the Holy Spirit who was given to us. (Rom. 5:3–5)

Granted, this may be hard to believe. There may be circumstances that prompt us to ask: How can anything good come of this? In these times, our lives need to be anchored in the promises of God's Word. No matter how bad things may seem, no matter how momentous the mountains may be, the trials sovereignly placed on our paths are there for our good. It takes faith and trust in the good purposes of God to navigate them and be refined by the redeeming power of the Spirit.

There is an acknowledged mystery to suffering. The specifics of why God grants a particular period of suffering is often outside our knowledge. The purifying purpose of this period may only be seen in hindsight. However, in His Word, the Lord has peeled back the veil of mystery to give us a glimpse of His sovereign wisdom in specific circumstances that gives us insight into His purposes.

## JOB AND JOSEPH:
## TRIUMPH THROUGH TRIALS

Two lives in the Old Testament Scriptures exemplify the inevitable encountering of trials. These lives also demonstrate the purposes that are working through the kind intention of the Lord. In these instances, the veil of mystery was removed for our benefit. In God's mercy, we are taken on a tour of the how He uses the direst of situations to demonstrate His glory and restoring power.

The name of Job has become synonymous with suffering. In the heavenly courts, the Lord pointed out to Satan a man of righteous living. No one was like him throughout the earth. The man's name was Job. Through the permission of the Almighty, Satan was able to ravage Job's life. Satan destroyed Job's family. He destroyed Job's possessions. He destroyed Job's health. The only explicit parameter was that Satan could not take Job's life. Throughout most of the narrative, Job struggles to find reasons for his extreme suffering. He is invited by his wife to curse God and die. He is admonished by his friends to repent, for surely this calamity must be due to some unconfessed sin. Job stood steadfast, refusing to curse God while remaining perplexed by the purpose of it all.

The Lord of Hosts arrived at the scene: "Then the Lord answered Job out of the whirlwind and said, 'Who is this that darkens counsel by words without knowledge? Now gird up your loins like a man, and I will ask you, and you instruct Me! Where were you when I laid the foundation of the earth? Tell Me, if you have understanding'" (Job 38:2–4). The Lord proceeds to

146

announce His sovereignty, His power, and His knowledge. He systematically demonstrates that He alone is the wise, Sovereign Ruler.

After going before the Judge of all, Job responds:

> "I know that You can do all things, and that no purpose of Yours can be thwarted. 'Who is this that hides counsel without knowledge?'

> "Therefore I have declared that which I did not understand, things too wonderful for me, which I did not know."

> 'Hear, now, and I will speak; I will ask You, and You instruct me.'

> "I have heard of You by the hearing of the ear; but now my eye sees You; therefore I retract, and I repent in dust and ashes." (Job 42:1–6)

Notice that Job is never actually given the reason for His suffering. All we know is that those who were "comforting" and advising him were declared to be in error (42:7) and that, at the end of the Job's sovereignly defined period of suffering, the Lord overwhelmingly restored his fortunes.

Yet when Job went before the holy, sovereign Lord, he did not declare "I understand." He declared "I *repent*." When we encounter the fullness of God's presence, I imagine our experience will be much the same. In the account of Job, the suffering children of God throughout the ages are given a glimpse of the unquestioned sovereignty and goodness of God. As the Scripture says, "We count those blessed who endured. You have heard of the endurance of Job and have seen the outcome of the Lord's dealings, that the Lord is full of compassion and is merciful" (James 5:11).

Another shining example of purpose in the midst of suffering is found in the story of Joseph. Joseph was one of Jacob's twelve sons. He was one of the chosen ones of Israel, being descended from Abraham, Isaac, and his father Jacob. He was one of His father's favored, inciting his brothers' envy and jealousy. They faked his death by taking his coat of many colors and dipping it in animal's blood and then sold him into slavery.

The story does not stop there. After Joseph was sold into slavery, he was wrongly accused and convicted of a crime he did not commit. He spent several years unjustly imprisoned.

All of these painful events were guiding Joseph to a glorious destination. God eventually delivered Joseph from the trials that burdened him. He rose to power in the land where he was once a slave. When guided circumstances caused his brothers to come to Egypt and fall under his authority, Joseph had the opportunity to take his revenge. Instead, when he was humbly approached by the very same brothers who had wronged him, Joseph gave the following response: "Do not be afraid, for am I in God's place? As for you, you meant evil against me, but God meant it for good in order to bring about the present result, to preserve many people alive" (Gen. 50:19–20).

The viscous acts of his brothers were intended by them for evil, but God intended them for good— for the preservation of life. The preservation was not only to save Joseph's family by providing for them in the midst of famine, but Joseph and his brothers resided in Egypt, which ultimately set the stage for the grand event of the Exodus through which the Lord declared all the nations would see His glory. This served as a shadow for the ultimate preservation of life found in Jesus Christ. All because of brothers' envy!

Job and Joseph are shining examples of how the Lord uses suffering and trials to accomplish His purposes and refine His people. Both of these patriarchs suffered a myriad of events that, at the time, had no good explanation. Now we behold the reasons through the unveiling counsel of God and can see how the Lord crafted these events for good. The redeemed of all the ages have been able to look to these trials in light of their ultimate conclusions and be fueled to brave the paths before them.

## THE ULTIMATE EXAMPLE

The power of the Lord to work out His purposes and to bring His glory out of seemingly gratuitous evil finds no greater example than at the cross of Jesus Christ. There was never a greater evil in the history of the world perpetrated by humans. The perfectly innocent Son of God, the Creator of all, was delivered up by His creation to be executed. The perfectly righteous Giver of Grace experienced brutal torture, irreverent mocking, and execution on a tree by three large spikes. Yet, the sovereign wisdom and good purpose of God was behind this event. Peter announces this truth by proclaiming:

> Men of Israel, listen to these words: Jesus the Nazarene, a man attested to you by God with miracles and wonders and signs which God performed through Him in your midst, just as

> you yourselves know—this Man, delivered over
> by the predetermined plan and foreknowledge
> of God, you nailed to a cross by the hands of
> godless men and put Him to death. But God
> raised Him up again, putting an end to the
> agony of death, since it was impossible for Him
> to be held in its power. (Acts 2:22–24)

God caused the greatest good to come out of the greatest evil. Through the cross, though godless men put His Son to death, God's predetermined plan was at work in reconciling the constituency of the kingdom and the cosmos itself from curse and corruption. In beholding God's sovereign wisdom and purpose behind the execution of His Son, how much more should we have confidence that He can, and will, work His marvelous grace through the trials of our lives?

## ASSESSING OUR OWN LOT

In the eighteenth century, Thomas Boston penned a timeless work on suffering in the believer's life. It was titled *Crook in the Lot.* In the introduction to a recent edition of this work, J. I. Packer defines the intent of the title. The "usage of the word *crook* is the crooked, that is the uncomfortable discontenting aspects of a person's life . . . (the) losses and crosses, and that we speak of as the stones in our shoes, the thorns in our beds, the burrs under the saddle, and the complaints we have to live with; and the lot is the providentially appointed path that God sets each of his servants to travel."[2] So we all have our own "crook in the lot." We all have various unpleasantries that cross our path. Each crook that finds its way into our lot is not there by accident, nor is there for our ruin. It is designed to purify us. It is our Father using the expansive resources He has to discipline His children. Note Boston's wisdom regarding this:

> God keeps the choice of every one's crook to himself; and therein he exerts his sovereignty (Matt. 20:15). It is not left to our option what that crook shall be, or what our particular burden; but, as the potter makes of the same clay one vessel for one use, another for another use, so God makes one crook for one, another for another, according to his own will and pleasure, 'Whatsoever the Lord pleased, that did he in heaven and in earth' (Ps. 135:6). He sees and observes the bias of every one's will and inclination, how it lies, and wherein it especially bends away from himself, and consequently wherein it needs the special bow.[3]

We need not, nor should we, devote ourselves *to* suffering. The purifying paths of suffering and the reasons for them are left in the hands of God, and God alone. We do not choose our mode and degree of discipline—He does. We are the children. He is the Father. The mere fact the He does discipline us is reason for rejoicing. We read in Hebrews:

> For those whom the Lord loves He disciplines, and He scourges every son whom He receives. It is for discipline that you endure; God deals with you as with sons; for what son is there whom his father does not discipline? But if you are without discipline, of which all have become partakers, then you are illegitimate children and not sons. Furthermore, we had earthly fathers to discipline us, and we respected them; shall we not much rather be subject to the Father of

151

spirits, and live? For they disciplined us for a short time as seemed best to them, but He disciplines us for our good, that we may share His holiness. All discipline for the moment seems not to be joyful, but sorrowful; yet to those who have been trained by it, afterwards it yields the peaceful fruit of righteousness. (Heb. 12:6–11)

We all have different temptations and that continually beset us, and we all have various trials that cross our paths to purify us. Our response is not to seek out suffering, nor is it to despair. We are to faithfully endure the fire that is sent to refine us, knowing that our gracious Lord is using this conform us to the image of Jesus. We must realize His goal for us is greater than our own. His chief purpose is for us to become conformed to the image of His Son.

Through the fire of trials, God causes all things to work together for good—that is, "good" defined by God and not by our shortsighted goals and desires. Note the promise in Romans:

And we know that God causes *all things to work together for good* to those who love God, to those who are called according to His purpose. For those whom He foreknew, He also predestined to become *conformed to the image of His Son.* (Rom. 8:28–29, emphasis mine)

## A PRODUCTION OF GLORY

In light of these truths, we must not be surprised when suffering comes our way. It is our "lot" until we enter glory. Suffering in the believer's life is far from a sure-fire sign of displeasure from God. Rather, it is sign of being one of His children. Through the suffering and trials the Lord sends our way, our association with the eternal gospel is shown and we experience the loving discipline that only belongs the children of the Most High. With these truths undergirding us, we can rest in the fact that our afflictions are guiding us towards an eternal, blissful goal. We are encouraged by the fact that "momentary, light affliction is producing for us an eternal weight of glory far beyond all comparison" (2 Cor. 5:7).

While we are on this side of glory, we may have difficulty grasping how this is so. But where were we when the Lord laid the foundations of the world? He has our ultimate goal and best interests in mind. Therefore, may we endure the road laid before us, trusting in the one who is working all things together for the good of those who love Him. He has provided the all-sufficient Shepherd of our souls, who is surely guiding us to glory.

---

[1] C. S. Lewis, *The Collected Works of C. S. Lewis* (New York: Inspirational Press, 1996), 464.

[2] J. I. Packer, "Introduction" in: *Thomas Boston, Crook in the Lot* (Ross-shire: Christian Focus Publications, 2002), 8.

[3] Ibid., 68.

For you were continually straying like sheep, but now you have returned to the Shepherd and Guardian of your souls.

1 Peter 2:25

11

# The All-Sufficient Shepherd

*Resting in the Savior's Ability to Provide*
*For Our Every Need*

"The Lord is my shepherd, I shall lack nothing" (Psalm 32:1).

What a robust declaration of the sufficiency that we have in Christ!

*Sufficiency.* This is one word with which every Christian needs to become intimately acquainted. When we truly understand the rich treasure that resides in Jesus' proclamation, "My grace is sufficient for you" (2 Cor. 12:9), an essential attitude will take root in our souls.

Just what is the treasure residing in this term, *sufficiency*, and why is it so important to have deeply planted in our souls? It holds the truth that we have been given the gift of an eternal Shepherd who will always meet our every need.

## OUR PROMISED SHEPHERD

Those who were entrusted with the care and
supervision of the children of Israel had failed. The
leadership had become corrupt and the nation was
driven to exile by the will of God. Even though the
covenant people of God were scattered, however, the
Lord of Hosts promised that, one day, He Himself
would come and remedy the situation. He would
arrive and shepherd all of His people from the ends of
the earth, and all ages, and gather them under His
tender mercy and grace.

> For thus says the Lord God, "Behold, I Myself
> will search for My sheep and seek them out. As
> a shepherd cares for his herd in the day when
> he is among his scattered sheep, so I will care
> for My sheep and will deliver them from all the
> places to which they were scattered on a cloudy
> and gloomy day. (Eze. 34:11–12)

When the true, promised Shepherd came, He
proclaimed that the time prophesied by Ezekiel had
come:

> "I am the good shepherd; and I know My own,
> and My own know Me . . . And I have other
> sheep, which are not of this fold; I must bring
> them also, and they shall hear My voice; and
> they shall become one flock with one
> shepherd." (John 7:14–16)

Jesus' voice is calling to the one flock, the community
of the redeemed throughout the ages. He doesn't
sleep. He doesn't get distracted. We are never outside
the realm of His watchful eye. He will never fail. We
have one Shepherd who is faithful and will not allow

us any of His sheep to perish. Peter includes all the redeemed in this promise: "For you were continually straying like sheep, but now you have returned to the Shepherd and Guardian of your souls" (1 Peter 2:25).

As we immerse ourselves in Jesus' teaching regarding His commitment to our care, our restless souls are set at ease.

## WHO CAN BE AGAINST US?

"Truly, truly, I say to you, I am the door of the sheep" (John 10:7), declares the Chief Shepherd. At first glance, this statement is somewhat peculiar. How is our Shepherd also the door?

In the first-century world, the shepherd was entrusted with his flock. So that his flock would enter the fold where they would be safe, the shepherd would call—his flock would hear his voice—and, recognizing him as their keeper, would proceed through the door to safety. In order to ensure no sheep would escape and no thief would enter in, the shepherd would lie down in the doorway, thus becoming "the door." Jesus being our shepherd and the "door" of the sheep signifies His all sufficiency in securing the salvation of His flock.

In the same context, Jesus notes that the security of the sheep that are given to Him rests not in their ability, but His:

> "My sheep hear My voice, and I know them, and they follow Me; and I give eternal life to them, and they will never perish; and no one will snatch them out of My hand. My Father, who has given them to Me, is greater than all;

and no one is able to snatch them out of the
Father's hand. (John 10:27–29)

Hearing Jesus' voice is synonymous with hearing and
heeding the gospel call to repent and trust in God's
provision. What Jesus so poetically establishes in this
passage, Paul reaffirms in the book of Romans.
Following the climax of Paul's declaration that all
upon whom God has set His love will be conformed to
the image of Christ, the apostle gives a rapid
succession of rhetorical questions that reveal the
depths of the Father's love:

> What then shall we say to these things? If God
> is for us, who is against us? He who did not
> spare His own Son, but delivered Him over for
> us all, how will He not also with Him freely
> give us all things? Who will bring a charge
> against God's elect? God is the one who
> justifies; who is the one who condemns? Christ
> Jesus is He who died, yes, rather who was
> raised, who is at the right hand of God, who
> also intercedes for us. (Rom. 8:31–34)

Take some time to really reflect on these statements,
as they sing of God's immense love for His children
and unrelenting grace in our lives: "I am the good
shepherd; the good shepherd lays down His life for
the sheep" (John 10:11). The Father sent the Son to die
a torturous death in order to bring us to Him. Since
He went to this length to secure us, we must realize
that He is delighted to freely give us all things. All that
He *has given* is overwhelmingly sufficient. All that He
*will give* is beyond our comprehension. He raised the
Lamb to become our eternal Shepherd, guiding us
through this life and leading us to the next. Now our
Shepherd ever lives to intercede for us. Therefore,

nothing can separate us, as His intercession will always be effective. This is a truth that is an anchor for the soul: "He is able also to save forever those who draw near to God through Him, since He always lives to make intercession for them" (Heb. 7:25).[1] This gospel truth leads to a song that every child of the King can rightfully sing:

> Who will separate us from the love of Christ? Will tribulation, or distress, or persecution, or famine, or nakedness, or peril, or sword? Just as it is written, "For Your sake we are being put to death all day long; we were considered as sheep to be slaughtered." But in all these things we overwhelmingly conquer through Him who loved us. For I am convinced that neither death, nor life, nor angels, nor principalities, nor things present, nor things to come, nor powers, nor height, nor depth, nor any other created thing, will be able to separate us from the love of God, which is in Christ Jesus our Lord. (Rom. 8:31–34)

God has given us the most precious gift of all: His own Son. He is the Lord of all, the one who justifies, and the one who condemns. Our verdict has been read at the cross. *Forgiven.* Since His Son endured the cross, we can rest in the knowledge that there is no power that can pluck us out of His grip. The Scriptures leave no room for anything else. If Christ is your Shepherd, then you may rightly stand in this truth as your eternal inheritance.

## SUFFICIENCY IN HIS PROVISION

Not only do we have a Shepherd who continually watches over and guards us, but He perpetually provides us with what we need in our continuing walk. We can continually devote ourselves to the apostles' teaching, to fellowship, to the breaking of bread, and to prayer precisely because He sovereignly extends these sufficient provisions for life and godliness. We already have all that we need in Him and the means to know His power. To repeat the truth from Colossians: "For in Him all the fullness of Deity dwells in bodily form, and in Him you have been made complete" (Col. 2:9–10). Peter further highlights this truth, writing, ". . . seeing that His divine power has granted to us *everything pertaining to life and godliness*, through the true knowledge of Him who called us by His own glory and excellence" (2 Peter 1:3, emphasis mine).

We are complete. We have been granted everything pertaining to life and godliness. These are the things in which the Chief Shepherd has commanded us to walk. The problem is not that He has failed to provide them; the problem is our fallen perceptions. We are sheep. We are prone to wander from the straight and narrow path. Therefore we must heed the call to not grow weary. It is a temptation to forsake that which is not a quick fix. Rather we are to listen to our Shepherd's voice through devotion to His Word. We are to communicate with our Shepherd through prayer, as He will grant us His refreshing and sustaining grace. We are to keep with the flock through fellowship, fixing our ever-wandering eyes to our magnificent Shepherd. As we devote ourselves to God's chosen provisions, His sufficient power will sanctify and secure us. Therefore, rather than grumbling or forsaking the incomprehensible gifts of grace, we are to be content in His sufficiency.

## "MY GRACE IS SUFFICIENT"

A grand lesson is given in sufficiency when Paul informs us of a great trial in his life. The Lord had allowed crook to enter his lot, leading him to so much distress that this apostle, already acquainted with much grief, was moved to exclaim: "Concerning this I implored the Lord three times that it might leave me" (2 Cor. 12:8). As far as we know, Paul's thorn was not removed, despite his pleadings. He was given a much better promise: "My grace is sufficient for you." Many have speculated on what exactly Paul's thorn was. Some have suggested it was sexual temptation, others poor eyesight. Various commentaries offer an array of postulations. However, I think the specificity of Paul's thorn has been intentionally withheld from us. We don't know what Paul's thorn was, but we know our own thorns all too well. Whatever our trials or temptations may be, His grace is sufficient to uphold His sheep and enable us to persevere. The promise is evident when we are thus encouraged:

> No temptation has overtaken you but such as is common to man; and God is faithful, who will not allow you to be tempted beyond what you are able, but with the temptation will provide the way of escape also, so that you will be able to endure it. (1 Cor. 10:13)

This text does not give us some esoteric, mysterious way that the Lord will reveal later, but rather establishes what and who has already been provided. Paul does not say *a* way but uses the definite article, *the* way. Our path through trails and temptations, and any other kind of evil, will perpetually be through "the Way, the Truth, and the Life" (John 14:6). He has secured us by His redeeming power, provided us with the sure promise of eternal redemption, and granted us His Word, fellowship, and prayer as continuing devotions that sustain us as we fix our eyes on the great Shepherd. When we behold such blessings to straying sheep, we can rest in the proclamation, "My grace is sufficient."

## RESTING IN HIS SUFFICIENCY

I can remember talking with a Christian who had come to the point of truly appreciating the promise of sufficiency through his many troublesome experiences. He said, "I love the truth of sufficiency now, but when a pastor first told me about it, I wanted to punch him in the face." Although perhaps not as extreme, this is a common first reaction to being told, "It is enough."

Hearing the declaration of the sufficiency of Christ may at first sound like something "less than." When we are told we have everything we need, our fallen inclination is to desire more. We want our thorns and temptations removed *now*. Thus, we may (and very wrongly so) take "My grace is sufficient" as a disappointment. In reality, His sufficiency is the source of rest and renewal for all who abide in Him. In the midst of the trials and temptations that test our faith, we look to our sovereign Shepherd, knowing that nothing can move out us out of His realm of grace. It is *always* enough.

No matter what comes our way, no matter how high the temperature of the fire, no matter dark it gets in the valley of the shadow of death, we take refuge in His protective and sustaining power. We rightly rest in proclaiming, "Your rod and your staff they comfort me" (Psalm 23:4). In trouble, in joy, in pain, in health, in life, and in death, His grace is always sufficient for His sheep. Knowing this will soothe our souls in times of trouble. By fixing our souls on that sufficiency, we will truly understand what this means: "He makes me lay down in green pastures. He leads me beside still waters. He restores my soul" (Psalm 23:2–3).

## Carrying Us to the Kingdom

While our Shepherd is surely giving us our daily bread and protecting us from the lurking wolves, He laid His life down in order to bring us to glory. The place to which our Shepherd is leading us is one our minds can scarcely contemplate. Yet this future is simply history that has yet to transpire. The book of Revelation gives us a sneak peak of this glorious day. In speaking of the sheep, it says: "For the Lamb in the center of the throne shall be their shepherd, and shall guide them to springs of the water of life; and God shall wipe every tear from their eyes" (Rev. 17:7). Jesus of Nazareth has picked up His sheep, placed us around His neck, and is carrying us to the kingdom. There we will drink eternally of the springs of the water of life. We will feast in our King's courts. Each step moves us closer to this joyful existence. He is guiding us to the completion of the course. Resting in His secure, unbreakable grip, let us explore what awaits us and realize the foretaste we are already receiving.

---

[1] The theological thrust and importance of intercession is discussed more in depth in chapter nine, "The Ascended Anchor," in my aforementioned work *Eternal Scars*.

# THE ALL-SUFFICIENT SHEPHERD

For indeed while we are in this tent, we groan, being burdened, because we do not want to be unclothed but to be clothed, so that what is mortal will be swallowed up by life. Now He who prepared us for this very purpose is God, who gave to us the Spirit as a pledge.

2 Corinthians 5:4–5

12

# A Foretaste of Glory

*Our First Steps into the Eternal Pleasures of God*

In the conclusion to John Bunyan's epic allegory *The Pilgrim's Progress*, we join our traveling companions, Hopeful and Christian, as they are on the threshold of finishing their journey. They have climbed the Hill of Difficulty. They have endured the Valley of the Shadow of Death. They have encountered the Giant of Despair. They have escaped the Castle of Doubt. Now they are on the cusp of completing their journey. They are about to enter the Celestial City. As they approach, two shining men greet them. Prior to the trumpets announcing the pilgrims' arrival, the men give the traveling pilgrims a preview of their destination.

> "There," they said, "is Mount Zion, the heavenly Jerusalem, thousands upon thousands of angels and the spirits of righteous men made perfect. You are now going to the paradise of God, in which you'll see the Tree of Life and eat of the never fading fruits of it. And when you arrive there, white robes shall be given to you, and every day your walk and your talk will be with the King, even all the days of eternity. You'll not see there again such things as you saw when you

> were in the lower region upon the earth—that is sorrow, sickness, affliction, death, 'for the old order of things has passed away.'"
>
> The Shining Ones continued, "You are now going to Abraham, Isaac, and Jacob, and to the prophets, men whom God has taken away from the evil to come and who are now resting upon their beds. Each one walks in His righteousness."[1]

Imagine an existence that is free from any sinful thought or inclination. Imagine a state of being in which pain and suffering cannot even pierce one's consciousness. Imagine a kingdom in which it is impossible to taste anything of the curse again. Hard to contemplate, isn't it? We have never known anything but this existence that has been stained by sin. We are unable to conceive what such a blessed state is actually like. Yet for all who have believed in the person and work of Jesus Christ, this future life is secured and sure. Like the pilgrims of Bunyan's Progress, those whom God has placed on the pilgrim's path cannot be thwarted. No power in heaven or on earth can prevent them from completing the course.

The finish line awaits. All who have journeyed through the narrow gate at the calling of our glorious Father are destined to be carried across the finish line by our Shepherd and King. When our commission is consummated and the goal of our pursuit is realized, we, like Jesus, will experience *resurrection*.

## The Promised Finish Line

While the community of Christ has spanned the ages across tribes, nations, and tongues, in a matter of seconds all will collectively cross the finish line and the commission to conformity to the image of Christ will be fulfilled: "For the Lord Himself will descend from heaven with a shout, with the voice of the archangel and with the trumpet of God, and the dead in Christ will rise first. Then we who are alive and remain will be caught up together with them in the clouds to meet the Lord in the air, and so we shall always be with the Lord" (1 Thess. 4:16–17). This moment of glory is the culmination of the sovereign plan of God for His children.

Before time began, before one molecule was created, the Lord set His love on His children and planned the course of their salvation. In the midst of describing the wondrous inheritance that God's children have obtained, Paul outlines a precious chain of events that takes us from before the foundation of the world to the blessedness of eternity.

> For those whom He foreknew, He also predestined to become conformed to the image of His Son, so that He would be the firstborn among many brethren; and these whom He predestined, He also called; and these whom He called, He also justified; and these whom He justified, He also glorified. (Rom. 8:29–30)

Paul outlines a chain that, for every believer, is more precious than gold. Before time began, the Sovereign Lord of Hosts set His love upon you and planned your redemption. He sent His Son to atone for you

169

and sent His Spirit into your heart to take you from the wretchedness of the kingdom of this world to the blessed kingdom of His Son.

All who are loved and predestined before the foundation of the world are called, justified, and ultimately glorified. There are no stragglers who do not complete the course. Why? Because the Author of our salvation is also the Finisher. He who began a good work in the depths of our being will bring it to its completion (see Phil. 1:6).

Therefore, the commission, which had is origins before the foundation of the world and found its reality in our very lives, reaches its conclusion in the future reality of *glorification*. Glorification is the final crowning act of our salvation. In spiritual terms, it is synonymous with resurrection.

## THE FIRSTFRUITS OF THE RESURRECTION

Jesus of Nazareth is called the *firstfruits* of the resurrection. The imagery of "firstfruits" is rooted in the Jewish festival that marked the beginning of the spring harvest. When the harvest had become ripe, the choicest grains would be brought before the Lord. This served as both a representation of the whole harvest and a pledge or guarantee that the rest of the harvest would be realized in the days that followed. With this as the backdrop, Paul's explanation of the process of the resurrection comes alive.

> For since by a man came death, by a man also came the resurrection of the dead. For as in Adam all die, so also in Christ all will be made alive. But each in his own order: Christ the first

fruits, after that those who are Christ's at His coming. (1 Cor. 15:21–23)

Just as the choicest grains were brought before the Lord, guaranteeing that the rest of the harvest would follow, the resurrected Lord He goes before His Father, a sign guaranteeing that the rest of the harvest will be raised in victory.

Just what is the nature of this new life? It is *eternal*. Eternal speaks of its duration. It will never end. Life speaks of its quality. It will be unending joy, when God will pour out His inexhaustible grace through His Son. This is what awaits us at the finish line. This is the ultimate consummation toward which we are striving. It is far from an elusive prize. It is a reality surer than the rising and setting of the sun. God's commissioned children *will* finish the race. They *will* experience resurrection and all of its inherent glory. Through our faith, we can announce our participation with the same assurance the apostle did:

> I count all things to be loss in view of the surpassing value of knowing Christ Jesus my Lord, for whom I have suffered the loss of all things, and count them but rubbish so that I may gain Christ, and may be found in Him, not having a righteousness of my own derived from the Law, but that which is through faith in Christ, the righteousness which comes from God on the basis of faith, that I may know Him and the power of His resurrection and the fellowship of His sufferings, being conformed to His death; in order that I may attain to the resurrection from the dead. Not that I have already obtained it or have already become perfect, but I press on so that may lay hold of

171

> that for which also I was laid hold of by Christ
> Jesus. Brethren, I do not regard myself as
> having laid hold of it yet; but one thing I do:
> forgetting what lies behind and reaching
> forward to what lies ahead, I press on toward
> the goal for the prize of the upward call of God
> in Christ Jesus. (Phil. 3:8-14)

One day, we will be transformed into the glorious
likeness of Christ. Since He is raised, it is a guaranteed
that we will follow. We press on towards the sure prize.
Because such a glorious life awaits those who complete
the course, the questions dance through our minds:
What will the fullness of the kingdom of heaven be
like? What will we see? What will we do? While the
answers will not fully be known until we arrive, God in
His infinite mercy has given us a preview.

## ETERNAL ENDEAVORS

As we walk through this world, our emotions are in a
sea of conflict. We are full of unspeakable joy because
of the gracious promises we have been granted and
because of the renewing power already at work in our
lives. Yet we are burdened with the reality of this
world and its obstacles. We long for our eternal
dwelling. In 2 Corinthians 5, Paul describes the
believer's "groaning" for the end of our journey.

> For indeed while we are in this tent, we groan,
> being burdened, because we do not want to be
> unclothed but to be clothed, so that what is mortal
> will be swallowed up by life. Now He who
> prepared us for this very purpose is God, who gave
> to us the Spirit as a pledge. (2 Cor. 5:4-5)

The power that will transform our mortal bodies into eternal righteous dwellings is already at work. The Spirit is given as a pledge, a guarantee that immortality is awaiting us. He resides in us and is already applying the renewing work of the Messiah. The spiritual endeavors that have been outlined in this work are not temporary gifts. On the contrary, they are unending means by which we will experience the eternal pleasures of God. In proclaiming the purifying power of grace, John Piper writes:

> The promises of future grace are the keys to Christ-like Christian living. The hand that turns the key is faith, and the life that results is called living by faith in future grace. By *future* I don't merely mean the grace of heaven and the age to come. I mean the grace that begins now, this very second and sustains your life to the end of this paragraph. By grace I do not merely mean the pardon of God passing over your sins, but also the power and beauty of God to keep you from sinning. By faith, I do not merely mean the confidence that Jesus died for your sins, but also the confidence that God will "also with him freely give us all things (Romans 8:32)." Faith is primarily a future-oriented "assurance of things hoped for" (Hebrews 11:1). Its essence is the deep satisfaction with all that God promises to be for us in Jesus—beginning now![2]

For the believer in Christ, eternal life has already begun. The Holy Spirit is active, and His means of grace carry us to the glorious promises of our all-sufficient Savior. What we *will do* in eternity has *already been inaugurated* by the Spirit. In the Word of God, in prayer, and in true spiritual fellowship, we are receiving a foretaste of the glories of eternity.

The Lord has established that His Word will perpetually stand. His statues, the proclamation of His glory, and the testimony of His Son are founded forever. When reflecting upon the Word of God, King David sang of the unending nature of the Lord's precepts:

> Your word, O Lord, is eternal; it stands firm in the heavens.

> Your statutes are forever right; give me understanding that I may live.

> Long ago I learned from your statutes, that you established them to last forever.

> (Psalm 119:89, 44, 152)

We have the gift of growing in His grace through His written Word. Yet our experience of the Word of God will be revolutionized when we enter glory. The wisdom of the Word, the truth of the Lord, and the glories of God are centered upon one—the Word made flesh. As we proceed through eternity, we will be walking with the Righteous One, Himself. We will be placing ourselves at His feet as He continues to take us into the depths of the glory of God. Our growth in the grace of God through feeding upon His inspired Word is a foretaste of our eternal inheritance. Heaven and earth may pass away, but His words will never pass away.

In the radical endeavor of prayer, we are going before the throne of God. We indeed communicate with God this side of the kingdom. However, when our King comes and consummates His work in us, this relationship will be revolutionized. Rather than communicating across the "great divide," we will see Him face to face:

> Now we see but a poor reflection as in a mirror; then we shall see face to face. Now I know in part; then I shall know fully, even as I am fully known. (1 Cor. 13:12)

*Face to face.* We will know fully the intimacy and radical relationship with our King. No longer will our relationship with Jesus be in part, but as Moses spoke with the Lord face to face, so will we. What will be our lot in eternity? We will be praising our King. We will be worshipping at His feet. We will be joining the angelic chorus in singing, "Salvation belongs to our God who sits on the throne, and to the Lamb. Be blessing and glory and wisdom and thanksgiving and honor and power and might, be to our God forever and ever" (Rev. 7:10, 12). We will never tire of communicating with our triune God. This relationship will reach its full expression in eternity, where we will be completely and utterly walking by the Spirit. When we enter the Spirit-filled endeavor of prayer, we are taking the first steps of a relationship that will have no end.

As we seek to walk by the Spirit through devoting ourselves to fellowship, we are participating in the gathering of the eternal members of the kingdom. Through serving each other in the pattern that Christ has set, and through our gathering around our common salvation, we are being given a foretaste of eternity. However, once we enter into the "fullness of fellowship," there will be no friction, factions, or fights. Instead, it will be table fellowship with the redeemed of all the ages. Our Lord told us of the feast

175

where we will experience the gathering of Christ's redeemed ones:

> "I say to you that many will come from the east and the west, and will take their places at the feast with Abraham, Isaac and Jacob in the kingdom of heaven." (Matt. 8:11)

As His community, we will be feasting upon the glories of our God and His Christ. Together we will converse and marvel at the majestic King, who bears the scars that bought us all. When we gather today, we are receiving a foretaste of this feast.

## The Ages of the Riches of His Kindness

The table is being set. The mansions are being prepared. The one who created all the glories we behold in this world—majestic mountains, wondrous waterfalls, and the other glories of His workmanship—will spare no expense in the marriage of His Son. Above all created gifts, we will be with our marvelous King. As we embark upon the journey through His Word, as we pursue His mercy and grace through prayer, and as we gather together to fellowship around our common salvation, we are experiencing a foretaste of the eternal pleasures and glories of God. By pursuing the prize of sanctification—conformance to the image of Christ—we are experiencing the initial tastes of a feast that will have no end. It was to this end that we were united with our eternal Savior.

> But God, being rich in mercy, because of His great love with which He loved us, even when we were dead in our transgressions, made us

alive together with Christ (by grace you have been saved), and raised us up with Him, and seated us with Him in the heavenly places in Christ Jesus, so that *in the ages to come He might show the surpassing riches of His grace in kindness toward us in Christ Jesus.* (Eph. 2:4–7, emphasis mine)

In light of His enduring kindness and the unending rest and refreshment awaiting the sojourners, may we grasp His gracious means of sanctification. Through the enabling power of the King, let us progress on the pilgrim's path and be conformed to the image of Christ. Our arrival is already accomplished. Nothing can prevent our destiny from being realized. With such promises laid before us, may we march forth in the Spirit of the living God, for we "are being transformed into his likeness with ever-increasing glory, which comes from the Lord, who is the Spirit" (2 Cor. 3:18).

---

[1] John Bunyan, *The Pilgrim's Progress* (Orlando: Bridge Logos, 1998), 206–207.

[2] John Piper, *The Purifying Power of Living by Faith in Future Grace* (Sisters: Multnomah, 1995), 13.

# About the Author

Ryan Habbena is the pastor of preaching and teaching at Conquering King Fellowship in St. Paul, Minnesota. He is also the director of Signet Ring Ministries, a biblical teaching and resource ministry. Ryan holds two degrees in Biblical and Theological studies (B. A. Bethel University, M. A. Bethel Seminary [New Testament]). Ryan lives with his wife and three children just outside of St. Paul, MN.

For more resources from the
ministry of Ryan Habbena go to:

# SIGNET
# R✝NG
## MINISTRIES

signetringministries.org

---

## CONQUERING
# K✝NG
## FELLOWSHIP

ckfellowship.org

www.ingramcontent.com/pod-product-compliance
Lightning Source LLC
Chambersburg PA
CBHW072046080426
42733CB00010B/2010